A Season of Wing-Shooting

A Season of Wing-Shooting

Hunting Tales from Washington State

To my Shawn...
Buddy Shawn...
Thanks for letting me skip work to kill birds, all those years ago.

John R. Otto III
Illustrator—Chris Engelhardt

Copyright © 2007 by John R. Otto III.

Library of Congress Control Number: 2007904889
ISBN: Hardcover   978-1-4257-8935-0
        Softcover   978-1-4257-8923-7

All rights reserved. No part of this book may be reproduced or transmitted in any form or by any means, electronic or mechanical, including photocopying, recording, or by any information storage and retrieval system, without permission in writing from the copyright owner.

Cover Photography
Jason Otto

Foreword Written by
Captain David Drewry

Epilogue Written & Illustrated by
Jason Otto

Edited By—Todd E. Costello

This book was printed in the United States of America.

To order additional copies of this book, contact:
Xlibris Corporation
1-888-795-4274
www.Xlibris.com
Orders@Xlibris.com

Contents

Foreword: Captain Dave Drewry 11
Introduction 13

Chapter 1:   Grouse Covers 19
Chapter 2:   Scouting for Doves 23
Chapter 3:   Early Season Salt Geese 30
Chapter 4:   Band-Tail Pigeons 36
Chapter 5:   Waterfowl Opening Day Weekend 44
Chapter 6:   Pheasants, Dogs and My Hero 60
Chapter 7:   Banded Barrows and Rough Seas 66
Chapter 8:   A Brothers Challenge 72
Chapter 9:   Teal Hunting Samish Bay Style 80
Chapter 10: Ringnecks and Ice on Emery's Ponds 85
Chapter 11: A Daughters First, a Dogs Last 90
Chapter 12: Marina Mallards 98
Chapter 13: The Mighty Merganser 104
Chapter 14: Snow Birds 110
Chapter 15: Canvasback Opener 118
Chapter 16: Lost at Sea 126
Chapter 17: The Christmas Goose 132
Chapter 18: Brant on Samish Bay 140
Chapter 19: Oldsquaws in the Layout 148
Chapter 20: Beach Hunting Bills 153

Epilogue: Jason Otto 163

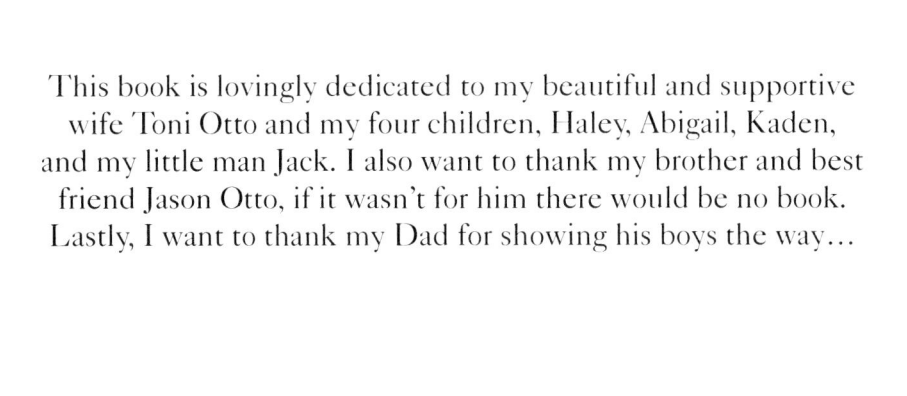

This book is lovingly dedicated to my beautiful and supportive wife Toni Otto and my four children, Haley, Abigail, Kaden, and my little man Jack. I also want to thank my brother and best friend Jason Otto, if it wasn't for him there would be no book. Lastly, I want to thank my Dad for showing his boys the way…

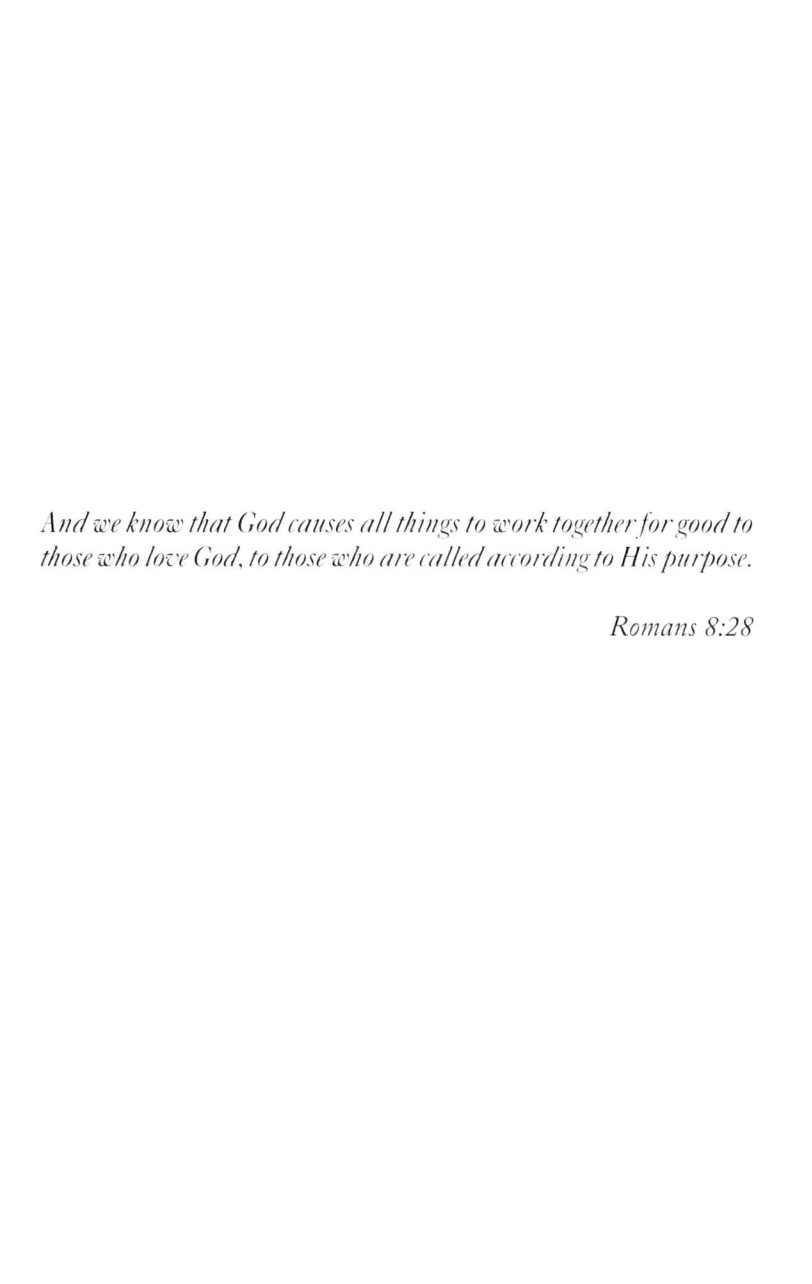

And we know that God causes all things to work together for good to those who love God, to those who are called according to His purpose.

Romans 8:28

Foreword

Captain Dave Drewry

Nothing sets my heart racing faster than a predawn launch. The duck boat loaded to the hilt with gear and decoys. The allure of a reddish golden sunrise over the ever changing waters of the Puget Sound. And the slow awakening of all our assorted sea ducks, divers, puddlers and geese. Stirred to the wing by their morning hunger, they seek the abundant food resources of the Puget Sound region.

Our fertile salt marsh and estuary environments, chock full of shellfish, eelgrass and other great duck delicacies, lure waterfowl on their migratory paths from their breeding areas to the North. Some birds will pass briefly through our state on the way to other wintering areas to the south. A majority, though, will find our temperate environments well suited for the duration of winter. These birds will take refuge here until the breeding urge lures them again to their historic breeding areas of Alaska and Northern Canada.

Waterfowling, to me, has become a rich mixture of the history and tradition. Here, we have combined the styles of the inventive, turn of the century market gunners of Chesapeake Bay, and the resilient Nor—Eastern

'Mainers. Toss in our own, unique hunting style, and you have a blended approach which is well suited for the diverse hunting here in the Pacific Northwest.

My seasoned crews have launched Duck boats of all shapes, sizes, and functions. These have all been loaded to the hilt with hand carved, modified, burlapped, and painted decoys of many local species. This, combined with our extensive rigging systems of longlines and clips, occasions the thought that we could rival the entire Pacific fishing fleet.

The reality is that one hunter can ply the quiet waters of Puget Sound for only so long before running into other sportsmen seeking similar quarry. Not that most of the diver and sea duck haunts have become over run with the sporting masses, far from it. But I had begun to appreciate the seclusion and freedom of not running into another boat in a days' hunting.

Several cold November's ago on a lonely spit off the Strait of Juan de Fuca, this would all change for me. That was the day I first ran into the Otto brothers. Two young men in a small green skiff were setting some familiar blue duck decoys in a special spot. One that for well over a decade I had considered "mine". Who did these guys think they were? I sat in the boat weighing my options. The fact that I am well acquainted with the remoter parts of the state seemed like it might come in handy.

As I was following this line of thought out, a voice kept suggesting that they had every bit the right to be there as I did. Hmm. Stupid conscience. Always interrupting a perfectly good revenge fantasy. Shelving my previous plans, I headed over to introduce myself.

The friendship and camaraderie that followed has become an important part of my and my family's lives. The adventures we have shared and the knowledge we have gained are all irreplaceable. Sharing that spot that day was well worth the price.

The following is a window into a wonder filled season of bird hunting with our good friends. John's dedication to the traditions of the past and his passion for the future of bird hunting are clear in the following chapters. Through his writing he has done an admirable job of capturing what we, as hunters and conservationists, appreciate and treasure about the resources of this unique part of the Country, along with the great times spent afield with friends and family.

Wings Locked!
Captain David Drewry

Introduction

Why Washington? Or more to the point, what does Washington State have to offer? It may be true that Washington does not enjoy the reputation or history that other areas across our country can claim, but it should. To my knowledge there are only a handful of outdoor heroes who have heralded this state as a major destination. When we think of big game the imagination wanders to the mountains of Montana, the wilds of Alaska, and the plains of Texas. Most Waterfowl hunters I know of dream about Maine, the Chesapeake Bay, the mighty Mississippi River, the flooded timbers of Arkansas, a Sacramento rice field, and even a Missouri cut corn field. When Uplanders drift into their areas of passion, the states of South Dakota, Nebraska or Iowa come to mind. And Washington? I like to think of my home state as a well kept secret, a place where all these other areas come together. Few in the Wing Shooting world have discovered that most of the game they share a passion for can be found right here.

When people think of Washington, their first thoughts are of coffee, the Space Needle, and yes, our ever occurring rain. Arrive here, and along with these there will be several other modern clichés, such as traffic and large chain stores. But what most folks do not realize is that our state is still quite rural. We may be fighting the battle against concrete each and every day, but what state isn't?

Our state is divided by the Cascade Mountain range, which creates two vastly different climates. The West side encompasses the Puget Sound, continues over to the peninsula, and then on to the Pacific Ocean. With a nod to our famous rain, this is known as the evergreen side. Head over towards the east side of the Cascades and you will discover mostly flat desert conditions. As you travel north to Canada the mountains ranges patiently begin to rise again. Living in Seattle you are always less than two hours away from desert, major rivers, mountains, ocean, bays, rain forests, and metro settings. We are richly blessed with diverse opportunities for the wing shooting enthusiast, making this is one of the most unique areas in the world for our sport.

For the Uplanders who like to hike through the covers while commanding their dogs to root through the bush, and cherish the explosion of sound as upland birds break the silence of nature, Washington has you covered. There are five types of Grouse to be found here, three of which can be hunted. The Blue, the Ruffed, and Spruce are all found in the foothills of the Cascade, Olympic, Blue, Okanogan Mountains and other wooded areas. While our Sharp-Tails are found in the Yakima Valley along with the Sage Grouse, they are protected as their numbers are too low to hunt. Ruffed Grouse hunting is the most talked about, but few people take the time to hunt them. Most harvests are usually incidental while deer hunting. And I don't know if the folks in Maine can say this, but when I hit the covers, I always find myself alone with thousands and thousands of acres all to myself. Please don't tell anyone about this!

I grew up a Pheasant hunter. Along with training dogs, this is my father's main passion. Growing up, the two naturally went hand in hand. As a result, I was fortunate enough to spend much of my youth behind great Labradors, and chasing the elusive rooster Pheasant. This bird holds a very special place in my heart.

Pheasant hunting is very popular here. While you cannot compare our state with the likes of South Dakota, on any given day you can be just as successful. Almost all of our Pheasant hunting is done on the East side of the Cascade Range, primarily in the Columbia Basin and East into Spokane or Walla Walla. On the West side all Pheasant hunting is on designated release sites, and is state funded, as the wet climate can not sustain a wild population. Our state has had many management issues over the years, with the current issue of funded "planting" now statewide being a major source of controversy. As the intent of this book is not political I will stay away from tackling any of the issue's of the day here, with the exception of saying I tend to hunt away from release sites.

There are two types of Quail hunting here, with the California species by far the most popular. While there are some scarce coveys to be found on the West side, most California Quail hunting is done in eastern Washington in much of the same habitat that you find Pheasants. The season here always starts a week or two ahead of the Pheasants and usually carries longer as well, giving the Quail hunter more opportunities. It would be tough to compare our Quail hunting with the likes of a Louisiana bottom wood, but our much hardier bird, when compared to the Bobwhite, is as plentiful as any where I have seen. The little known and hardly hunted Mountain Quail can be found in the foothills with some diligent scouting. Not very plentiful, and only recently legal to hunt, these magnificent birds are always a challenge. They are about the size of a Teal duck with a long, straight top notch. The first challenge is to find them, the second is the shot. The covey will bust in several different angles, just like the California, but they are mostly found in the forest. And for some reason a tree always finds a way to shield them. At least they do for me.

When you think of Doves, Arizona will spring to mind. Maybe even Texas or New Mexico. But Washington? You bet. At times we have flocks numbering in the thousands. There may be no way to compare the hunting to the above mentioned states, but I have been on hunts where the action is fierce and a ten bird limit can be measured in minutes. When you consider it takes at least two boxes of shells for your ten birds, you get my point. Again, Dove is primarily an eastern Washington hunt and the only species we get are Morning Doves. Not quite as big as the White-Wings, but just as sporty, and in my opinion one of the best tasting game birds to be found. Doves are hunted in September and the first bite of cold finds the masses migrated to warmer climates immediately. A good season is dependent on a nice hot summer keeping the birds in the Columbia Basin.

Another little known game bird found in the mountain areas in Washington is the Band-Tail Pigeon. This close relative of the extinct Passenger Pigeon migrates down the mountain chains from Vancouver Island to the warmer climates, much like the Dove. Band-Tails carry a long and controversial history in the Pacific Northwest and only recently have they been re-opening to hunting in Washington. Currently the decision to open the season is made on an annual basis, and by harvest permit only. The season is made up of seven days, and much like the Dove, success is based completely on the weather cooperating leading up to those seven days. I have had seasons of not seeing a single bird, and other seasons where a quick double at first light and my day is done in seconds. As you will find in this book, this wild bird is by far my most passionate to hunt. To experience the Band-Tail you will find yourself in some of our most remote, wild areas, full of rugged terrain that usually only Bears enjoy.

Our Chukar and Hungarian Partridges are also found in excellent numbers in the Eastern part of the state. In most hunting seasons I find myself running out of time to pursue these birds, but they are none the less important in our area. In our regulations they are lumped together as "gray partridges" and share the same season lengths as Quail. In the desert regions there are many hills and cliffs the Chukar call home. One of my favorite memories is when I was hunting a small lake that bordered a hill made up entirely of rock. Desert conditions were all around and the weather was very cold. My brother Jason and I were in a lakeshore blind, hunting Bluebills and Goldeneyes. Much of the lake had frozen over, making for an eerie quiet. About an hour after sunrise the Chukar on the hill began to call. The sounds echoed through the little valley the lake had created. They called the entire day, keeping my brother and me company in the vast wasteland we were visiting. I find it to be very soothing. Hungarians are found mostly in the lowlands, especially on the cut wheat fields of the Colfax or Pullman area in the very eastern part of the state. Unlike Chukar where you have to target them specifically, most of the Huns that make up my bag are shot while Pheasant hunting. They have salvaged many a long Pheasant hike for me, and they taste just as good.

Moving on to Waterfowl, both sides of the state can boast of plenty to offer the wingshooter. Most Waterfowlers cherish the Mallard above all other ducks and we possess some of the greatest greenhead shooting in the country.

From the Columbia River, over the agriculture fields of the Basin, to the Snake River, and on into the far corners of the state, the Mallard reigns supreme. This is well known in the Waterfowling community. What is not well known is the variety of the other ducks that inhabit our state. No where else in the lower 48 will you find such an astonishing amount of species. In the marshes you will find all the puddle ducks, the Gadwall, Wood Duck, Pintail, American Wigeon (and if your lucky, the European), Shoveler, GreenWing Teal, and to some degree, early in the season, the Cinnamon and BlueWing Teals. On our lakes, rivers and ponds you can chase Ringnecks, Lesser Scaup, Greater Scaup, Bufflehead, Ruddy Ducks, Canvasbacks, Redheads, Hooded Mergansers, and Common Mergansers. Out on the salt water you will find the Common Scoter, Surf Scoter, WhiteWing Scoter, Harlequin, Oldsquaw, Common Goldeneye, Barrows Goldeneye, and Red Breasted Merganser. I call these the "25 Species List" and every year I challenge myself to harvest them all.

There is no other area of the country where you can chase all these birds in their fall plumage. To top it off, we rarely hunt these birds on private property. Washington is one of those rare places where the public lands seem to be infinite. Granted, much of our agricultural areas are leased up, and the sprawl of civilization takes away more land every year, but there is still an amazing amount of acreage of public land. Much has been done to ensure this will never change, in the hope that our traditions will last many more generations. I sure came to appreciate this when I visited Texas, where even the mud puddles were leased!

Goose hunting is probably the pride of Washington State. The Canada goose is found throughout and is extremely plentiful. There are many freelancers and reputable guides here who are known world wide for offering first class goose hunting that rivals any state in the union. A large variety of sub-species can also be found, giving the collector much to strive for. Most notable are the Dusky, Cackler, Lesser, Richardson, Western, Vancouver, and the Aleutian. The Aleutians are now protected. They can frequently be spotted in the foothills, making it easier to separate and not confuse them with the others.

Also quite popular is the Snow Goose, which is primarily found on the West side. We do not have the Blue Goose that is normally found mixed in the Snows of the Central Flyway, but the occasional Ross has been harvested. Specklebelly geese come through early in the season on both sides of the state and are sometimes mixed in with the Canada's.

My personal goose of choice is the Pacific Black Brant and the Melville Island Gray Belly Brant. The season on these little sea geese changes from year to year, depending on population counts, and are regulated to only a few counties and small bays. Very few hunters consider these birds due to their limited target days and areas, but those of us in the know realize how rewarding a day on the salt water can be. I am a Director in the Washington Brant Foundation, and Brant are a primary passion of mine.

We live in the small town of Marysville. It is located about forty miles north of Seattle. I love living here because I am centrally positioned, with easy access to all areas of the state.

I have hunted in many states, and I have still not found a more diverse area in which to hunt. You will find I tend to lean towards more traditional approaches to the way I go about a hunt. As we attempt to harvest all our different species, you will see the many contrasting environments across the four corners of the state. I write not just about a variety of targets, but also about my relationships with those I am fortunate enough to share the cover or the blind with. I cherish the moments spent afield, and those I spend them with, be they dog or person.

I have had the same hunting partner since I was a young boy. Those that are lucky enough to know what it is like to have a long term hunting relationship know how rewarding it is to have this close bond. Jason Otto is my best friend in life and in the field. We are pretty much inseparable, and I wouldn't have it any other way. I also have a few lifelong partners along for the ride, with some great visitors that we have the pleasure of hosting from year to year. I am extremely lucky to have been raised by my father, who is also named John Otto. From an early age he brought my brother and me hunting whenever he had the chance. His guiding hand and exposure to the great outdoors passed on a passion that I will follow to the day they finally dig a hole and bury me. I in turn hope to pass this passion on to my own children and the generations to follow.

The following hunts are from the 2004-05 hunting season. I hope you will enjoy reading about our adventures as much as we did living them.

Chapter 1

Grouse Covers

 There is something about that first day. The off season is over. You have prepared all summer and now it is finally here. The night before I always toss and turn. I do this almost any night before a hunt, but for the first hunt of the year, the butterflies just seem more intense. That 4:00 am alarm hits hard for me, but I remind myself this is just one of a long series of mornings of getting up this early. By the end of the season I will be fantasizing about sleeping in, but not now. My wife Toni jumps right out of bed, tending to four children has made her a pro at this early morning thing. I stagger to the shower, more for a wake up than to actually clean myself. As I dry off I can smell the coffee brewing downstairs. This alone gets me jittery, as I only drink coffee during the hunting season. With the smell come many happy memories. Focus, I must focus . . .

I get dressed and go to my closet gun safe. Putting my shotgun into the scabbard gets me giddy. This time it is for real. No trap shooting or 5-stand for me today, those are only time wasters until we can get to the real deal. The gun of choice today is my old Winchester Model 97 pump. It was manufactured in 1914, and is still in incredible shape. I had searched after this one for years; I had always wanted one that actually worked. I don't care for guns that just hang on the wall. I need to use them. My Dad's first gun was a Model 97, and for me, having one also has a romantic appeal. My grandpa had gotten rid of my dad's gun after it accidentally discharged on a hunt in the early '60s. At the time it was a good decision, as these guns aren't known for their safety. I sure wish I had that gun today. I would definitely break my own rule and hang it in the trophy room. Every time I hold my own model 97, I wonder what memories it contains. I was told by the gunsmith that checked it out that it probably did not have too many. A gun that finds itself in this good of shape almost 100 years after it was made just did not get used that much.

I did not expect this. I strolled downstairs to discover Toni had eggs and bacon going. What a wife! Her constant kindness's keeps me smiling all day. She knew I thought that this was going to be the last day of hunting for one of my oldest and most cherished hunting partners, my Lab Comet. Comet was getting up there in age and I knew she did not have much more mileage left. Earlier in the year, in April, my Dad and I had gone to a pheasant reserve in Peck, Idaho (Little Canyons Reserve) for some rooster hunting. With us were Comet and her pup Teal. Teal is my Dad's dog, and at 9 years old is hardly a pup herself. Most of this hunt I had Comet by my side until she would catch scent. Watching her lying around for three days after the trip had me realizing it was time to retire her. I just could not bring myself to end her illustrious career at a reserve so I promised her one last day in the covers. Today was the day

I had loaded the truck the night before and was ready to go. Toni gave me a little peck on the cheek as I headed out the door. I could tell she was holding back a tear, and I was thankful. It was just too early in the day for that to start, and there would be plenty of time for it later. I walked to the back yard to round up Comet. I found her sitting by the gate waiting. It was funny, any other morning I would have had to of woken her up. I don't care what anyone says, dogs know when it's hunting time. After helping her into the kennel, I got in the truck and headed out.

It is about an hour drive up to the mountain, and then another half hour until we hit the covers. These are nestled deep into the Cascade foothills, just north of the small town of Whitehorse. It was opening day, and we were after Ruffed Grouse. I could hardly contain my excitement on the drive up. Ordinarily such a moment would not find me alone, but this day I found myself just that, alone. My regular partner, my brother Jason, is a golf course superintendent and this time of year is his busiest. The hotter it is, the more stressed he gets. We traditionally take off on Labor Day weekend for Dove, so in order for him to do this he has to prepare the course for the long weekend without him. September 1st is usually a planned casualty. I would have liked to share Comet's last day, but it was almost meant to be this way, just me and her.

 I was relieved to find the covers nice and dry, it had rained a bit earlier in the week and I was worried we would be washed out. The morning dew was perfect for scent. As I was getting ready, I couldn't wipe the smile off my face. Here I was, all alone, in the middle of no-where, and I just was just soaking it in. The way the shell vest slid right on over my shoulders, the sounds the shells made as they piled into the large pockets. I let Comet out of the kennel and you would have thought she was a puppy again. One of the strangest things about Comet is as she got older, she didn't gray. Most labs of her age have a gray chin and muzzle, not her, black as night. I kept her in good shape and people would not believe she was twelve years old. I kneeled down to give her a snuggle, and held her tight. I whispered a little prayer in her ear, something private for just me and her.

 Our first spot of cover was some waist high wild grasses at the edge of an old abandoned road that cut through some second growth timber. My heart pounded as I cut through the wandering twigs and fallen logs. I was hunting again! I almost didn't bring my whistle. It had been a long time since Comet needed reminding on the appropriate distances needed to quarter the area. In her excitement she quickly got out of range and had to be called in. It was a great sign to see her so agile. About a half mile in, I could see her tail wagging quickly. I knew she had caught scent. She worked the cover all the way to the edge of the trees, where her moves slowed down and became much more methodical. There was something there, and it was going to happen now. I moved in, but moved in too close. The Blue Grouse erupted from the cover and disappeared into the darkness of the trees before I could even get my gun up. There was just enough time to identify the bird. I quickly looked into the branches, as sometimes they will simply fly to the first available perch. Nothing! I had blown it; I hadn't given myself enough space to see anything. Comet just looked at me, as if to say, "Hey, we'll have more chances, right?" My once pounding heart had sunk deep into my stomach. Hunting grouse in the Pacific Northwest does not always guarantee another opportunity.

 About an hour later we hiked up a ravine to another old logging road. The cover was similar, but not as thick. This time the trees were from a clear cut only a few years old, nothing over ten feet high for about a quarter mile. We worked the edges for quite some time. I had almost thought the cover may be too thin when Comet darted off. As she zigzagged through, I saw a Ruffed Grouse run across the road. I ran to where I saw the bird only to be beaten by a hustling Comet. As soon as she hit the other side the bird flushed straight out, flying really low and heading right. I rose up and shot, pumped the old Model 97, and shot again. This time a puff of feathers burst out and I saw the bird fall down a steep cliff. Comet was already in tow, long had she forgotten the virtues of a "steady" dog, and headed down the cliff. Although I had yet to breathe because I was so excited, I ran in fear Comet would fall down an even larger cliff. My fears were quickly put to rest, as I got to the edge she was already heading up, with the bird in her mouth. She brought it to heel and I was holding a perfect example of a beautiful Ruffed Grouse.

All this excitement was just too much. I had to sit down. She lay dutifully by my side and I just absorbed it all in. From my seat I could see the entire valley, all the way to Darrington. The highway that cut through the woods had a few cars on it that seemed almost microscopic, I was up so high. I remember holding her in one arm, and the grouse in the other, still shaking. I couldn't help but drift back to all the memories we shared, both the good and the challenged. I thought of how perfect this day was turning out to be.

The rest of the morning Comet pretty much spent hiking by my side. Her age was showing and I couldn't wait to get her back in her kennel. We did pick up one more bird, not as memorable as the first, but exciting just the same. A Ruffed flushed from a tree, totally unseen by both of us. I was able to get one quick successful shot off before it disappeared into the trees. She made another remarkable retrieve in the thick blackberry bushes, our day was complete.

When we got back to the truck I just couldn't bear having her sitting in the kennel for her final ride home. I was raised by a strict dog trainer and rules were rules. Normally the thought of anything else would never have entered my mind. But this time was different. Up on the seat she went. Of course she slept the entire way home, except when I stopped for a snack. She loves Hostess Fruit Pies by the way. I had to carry her to her "inside" bed in the corner of the living room where she laid for the better part of four days. We would soon take off on our Dove hunting trip and it just wasn't going to be the same without her. This would be her last hunt, or at least I thought, and it had been a good one.

Chapter 2

Scouting for Doves

    Well, that didn't go as planned. For over 15 years I have made the same phone call, and have had the same results. This time it went quite different. This subject has been discussed and dissected a hundred times over by many a hunter. For the first time ever our farmer friend where we hunt Doves has decided to lease out his property. Not to bird hunters, but to Deer hunters. Dove hunting will spook the deer, he said, and he regrets we will not able to come over and use his property. As disappointed as I was, I could not deny the run of good fortune we had in those fields. There were many years of successful hunts, with great times and great friends. We had tried to tie the place up with a lease in the past, but he would always say he didn't want any money from hunting, it just didn't feel right to him. I guess he finally found the right "feeling", but don't they all? It was time to file that spot into the memory banks and move on.

    This called for "Plan B". The original plan was for Jason and our good friend Captain David Drewry to head out early Friday morning. Dave runs a local guide service, Peninsula Sportsman, where he caters to the outdoorsman in everything from fishing, hiking, crabbing, to his specialty of Sea Duck hunting. These trips are very special to me and Jason because with Dave being so busy during the hunting season with his clients, it is hard for us to squeeze in time with him. This gave me more determination to not accept that our trip was cancelled. I had a plan.

It was Thursday morning and the area of the Columbia Basin that we wanted to hunt was about four hours away. I quickly threw my gear in the truck, kissed Toni and my girls good-bye, and was on the road. While driving I called Jason and Dave and explained the situation. My goal was to get us some ground by nightfall, make camp, and be hunting in the morning. I had to follow that up with a hearty "trust me!" I wasn't sure how much faith they had in me, but the fact they were both coming in the morning was all I needed.

Scouting is difficult enough. But to do it hours away and at the last second is hardly ideal. In fact, there is nothing eastside residents of Washington detest more than the last second "206'er" coming over trying to push themselves on their land. The term 206 comes from the Seattle area code, which marks us as city slickers. I am hardly a city slicker, but my living even in the vicinity of Seattle can confirm their fears if I am not careful. And I don't blame them. Countless stories of hunters without any respect coming over from the west side and damaging farm equipment, hurting livestock, trespassing, and overall disregard for their property have unfortunately tagged a reputation on everyone who comes over the Cascade Mountain pass. For this reason I will not tolerate negative actions of other sportsmen, they represent us all, good and bad.

With all that in mind, my first stops were to hit a few farms that I had hunted at and were vaguely familiar with in the past. Spending as much time in that area as we had in the past twenty or so seasons, we were able to network a little bit. The problem was I hadn't talked with many of these people in as much as six or seven years. I was hoping they would remember me. Just north of the little town of Mesa, I pulled into a homestead we called Finger's Farm. That name really had nothing to do with anything other than the fact that Jason and I have nicknames for every place we hunt, and the old guy that used to run the place was missing most of his fingers. Most of the time I have no idea why or when we come up with some of the names, but they always seem to stick, even if the are a little strange.

The majority of his fields had gone back to CRP and sage and long ago he had leased to a club out of Bellevue, which is "206" city slicking heaven. They had a stand of trees the Doves flocked to in the afternoon and I knew this would be a great score. I noticed the signs were still up but looked really ragged. Hey, what the heck, I thought. The worst case scenario is just a "no," after all. I was greeted at the door by an elderly woman.

"Excuse me Ma'am, sorry to bother you, but I used to hunt this farm with my family years ago and would love to get permission to do this again?" I gave it all the charm I could muster.

"Oh dear, why of course you can! I remember you, isn't your father's name Rick?"

Oh man, yes! Success on the first door. Only problem, I have no idea who Rick is? But without skipping a beat I answered her.

"Oh yeah, Rick, I mean Dad, is doing great. In fact, he was planning on joining us but he is sick at home right now or I would have had him swing by."

This wasn't entirely false. My dad, whose name is also John, was going to join us but cancelled because he didn't feel good. Rick, John? Close enough for me. I thanked her kindly, asked her where we were able to drive and hunt, and moved on down the road. It seems the folks that had the lease had only paid for one year, and then walked away. I sure wish we had known that a few years ago. I knew this spot was going to produce, but it wasn't going to be enough. We still needed a morning shoot and most importantly a place to camp. Our old spot came complete with a perfect little area for dropping a few tents. There is nothing better than Dove camp, right in the middle of the action. I needed to replace our old slice of heaven.

Next up was a little farm that was relatively close to where we had recently lost our old spot. I was about to find out how close it really was. We had dubbed this Crazy David's Trailer Farm, or just plain "Crazies". We hadn't hunted there in years. All I remembered about this place was the owner. I think his name was David, funnily enough. He also used to hunt and liked to keep his place to himself. As I pulled into the driveway, I was met with two rapidly barking dogs showing all teeth. Yikes. I also had to avoid running over the garbage that was spread out all over the lawn, it was obvious I was interrupting the fun the dogs were enjoying. I slowly opened my truck door and was thankful when I heard the front door crash open.

"Dang dogs! Down!" He yelled as he leaped to grab them. I froze. The last thing I wanted was a trip to the emergency room.

"Sorry about that, can I help you?" he said while corralling the mangy mutts to their chain. He was also looking at the handy work of his pets with a look of disgust. All I kept thinking was great, this guy is really upset, and I don't recognize him at all.

"I hope I am not bothering you," I started out rather shakily, "but I am just out trying to secure some ground to hunt Doves. I used to hunt around here. Do you think it would be OK?"

He kind of looked at me. "Hunt Doves? Why?"

I felt I knew where he was going with his question. I assumed him to be a big game hunter. After all, why spend money and time if you can't fill your freezer right? "Well, I replied, good hunting, good eating, and good times with friends . . . do you hunt?" Instead of replying to my question, he just looked a little puzzled. He was of giving me a look like he had seen me before.

"Aren't you the guys that camp every year down at the old draw on Hilmes land?"

"That would be us!"

And that was that. The beginning of success for "Plan B". Turns out the fellow I was talking to was a renting the house on the land owned by David. Out of completely blind luck a few years earlier we had encountered David's wife after a hunt. She went on to tell her husband how nice the group of hunters were that camped every September down in Hilmes' draw. When this guy moved in, David had told him we would be down there and to let us have the run of his property if we were ever to ask. And of course we would ask, considering that a Dove hunt can sound a lot like World War three.

The property was directly lined up with our old spot on the west side. I was beginning to realize just how big of an area I had secured. He took me down to their side of the draw and showed me where we could camp. It was literally across the dirt road that divided the two properties. I couldn't believe our luck. On top of that we had a great afternoon spot only a couple of miles away. The hunt was on. We were now in better shape than before. Now, if only the Doves would cooperate.

I quickly ran into the town of Connell. I called Dave and Jason to tell them of the good news. While there I also bought my new friend a well deserved case of Bud Light, his beer of choice.

Much to my surprise, both guys were already on their way over. I told them both of my good fortune, and of course how lucky I was. I laughed at their attitude of complete faith in my scouting ability but I knew their early arrival was more of a response for the help I am certain they felt I needed.

The timing of their arrival could not have been more perfect. I was putting the last of my bags into my tent when I heard the hum of their trucks coming down the dirt road. Surrounding our camp were corn fields to the north, sage to both the east and west, and a peaceful water canal bordering the south. Perfect. I hadn't seen many birds yet, but I knew that in the evening they would be coming to the trees bordering the canal. As our crew arrived, I was hoping they would be up for the nicely unexpected beginning to our Dove season.

Knowing we had little time, the decision was made to catch the evening hunt and then to attempt to set up camp in the dark. We were there to hunt after all, and who can unpack while watching birds in the air? I could see the excitement in Dave's face and the lack of patience in Jason's. It had been a long drive for them. And for me it had been a long day, period. It was time to go. The guys gave me a quick little toast with water bottles to acknowledge the success of our spot. We grabbed our gear, watered the dogs, and set off. Considering we were now in a relatively new area we agreed to spread out to the corners to make sure we covered all the possible hot spots.

I chose the most southern area, right below one of the mature Russian Olive trees that bordered the canal. The wind had picked up a bit and it felt good. It had to be 90 plus degrees even with the sun winding down. The smell of the burnt wheat field on the other side of the canal made my eyes water. I looked away and wiped my eyes. When I looked back up, they were there. Thousands of swallows. They were dipping into the water and darting over my head. They had me completely surrounded. I started to get dizzy from watching them.

Bang! I quickly looked left to see Captain Dave had taken the first shot. Bay, his Chesapeake Bay retriever was in full retrieve. Our first bird of the trip. In our circle first bird earns him a dollar from each of us.

Dave's shot could have easily been a starting gun. The swallows seemed to get larger, and now mixed in were Doves, all around. They were coming in groups of two's, three's, and four's. I pulled up, emptied my gun, reloaded, shot three shells once again. Nothing! I could hear Jason in full shooting mode. Then Dave started again. The shoot was on. I was trying to shake the stink of rust off my shooting, and not doing it well. Finally, a lone customer came right at me. It looked as though it were decoying into a spread in the trees. I found out I was right. I took my shot, folding the bird. Out flushed about twenty doves that had sneaked into the trees on the back side. I used my remaining two shells to down another one. Ahh . . . that felt great.

I quickly ran out to retrieve my two birds. Since Comet was at home, probably sulking, I had to mark my own birds as well. The first was a perfect feathered Morning Dove. Right there I felt that all the work of the day had been worth the effort. With the shiny iridescence of the purple feathers around his head and the creamy textured underside of his belly, he was really quite remarkable. I hustled back to my perch and was quickly shooting again.

All in all it took us twenty five minutes for each to get our ten bird limit. We regrouped back at camp and the excitement was at an all time high. Hearing Jason talk about the bird he shot on his third attempt and Dave giving us a blow by blow of a triple he managed to accomplish was as satisfying as if I had done it. We were a team. The real stars of the night though were Bay and Ruddy. Bay dog being a Chesapeake is not quite what you would expect to see in the hot sage filled cover. You couldn't tell her that. She took to the alfalfa and corn stocks no different than if she was crashing into a half frozen December pond. I was amazed at how well she handled the heat. This was her first Dove hunt, taking over for her predecessor Marley, also a Chessy, who like Comet was in her first year of retirement. Last year both Marley and Comet gave Dave and me quite a scare. We were walking back from hunting a dirt field when Comet just sat down and would not get up, panting rapidly. While I was packing her in, Marley did the same thing. Lucky for us there was a small irrigation canal nearby where we were able to cool the dogs down. We both decided that would be their last hunt in the heat, at their age it was just too much.

Ruddy, still a relative pup was on her first Dove hunt as well. Jason had opted the year prior to not bring her for the same reason we weren't bringing the old dogs, the heat. This was hardly an issue this year, she looked invincible. Her ability to mark down birds was second to none and this saved a few Doves that had coasted or fell in thick cover. I even had to borrow her to help me find a couple of birds that I had failed to mark. It is amazing how such a colorful bird can blend into the dirt and dead grass. We didn't lose a single Dove.

While the guys set camp, I cleaned and prepared the birds, holding some out for our evening feast, fresh meat for the barbeque. Now, here are a few things about Captain Dave. He is a certified expert on the grill. More impressively, he knows what foods to bring to a hunt. Dave has adopted a lifestyle for him and his family where the meat on his table is the meat he harvests. He travels up and down the coast hunting wild boar, buffalo, deer, and elk. You name it and he hunts it. Eating at his house is always a treat, but eating with him in camp is half the fun of the trip. On the menu would be Moose burgers and wild boar dogs to go with the Dove. A meal fit for a King.

The next day we had to ration out our harvest. We decided to self limit ourselves to two birds each in the morning and then two birds in the afternoon. We had invited a guest for the evening shoot and there would be nothing worse for him than to have three guys just sit there and watch him do all of the shooting. Our guest was Mike Schmuck, a warm fish biologist for the state. He lives in Ephrata, which is about an hour and a half from our camp. He is a friend of ours, and we had told him if the shooting was good he should come on by and spend the evening with us. When we called to give him our report he informed that us that the day before he had shot a Dove on his property and that it had been banded. Excited to see the band we told him to hustle on out. I had never seen a Dove band but knew they were doing studies throughout the Basin. Maybe rubbing one for luck would work.

Mike arrived just in time to hit the fields for the evening go around. He brought along his Lab, Scout, who is quite the character. It is hard to explain, but that dogs face has the most serious intensity mixed with the goofiest looks I had ever seen. I decided I would hunt with Mike and Scout while Dave and Jason would take the other dogs to the opposite side of the draw. Experiencing the same flight as the night before, it didn't take long to once again fill our limits. A highlight of the evening was a Dove I shot that dropped in a pile of logs. The crippled bird buried itself deep into the mess of twisted branches and overgrown weeds. Scout circled the pile about ten times before digging in the surrounding dirt and squeezing into the center. After about ten minutes of some of the most violent thrashing Scout came barreling out of the snags, Dove in mouth. The whole experience was extremely exciting and we whooped that one up for hours.

We left the following morning after a quick hunt and seeing Mike off. It was the first time I had shared the field with him and I really enjoyed his company. The previous night had been a victorious celebration, with cold beers and plenty of excited talk of the upcoming waterfowl season. The Dove hunt always marks the beginning of the travel season for us and it sets the tempo for all the upcoming trips. This trip did not disappoint. More importantly, we secured a new area for Dove, a new beginning as it were. This would be the starting point of many memories for years to come.

Chapter 3

Early Season Salt Geese

    I have to start by saying that I do not consider myself a true goose hunter. The state of Washington is full of Waterfowlers whose number one passion is chasing the Canada goose. They will spend every available day scouting for that perfect place to put the blind. They will work hours on end perfecting the call of their choice, and are more than willing to spend thousands of dollars on all of the custom decoys that have surfaced over the last couple of years. Then they have to flock them all. And then, well, you get my point. Some of the more well known goose hunters in our state would be Ben Holten, Billy MacDonald, and Troy Wiley of North Flight Waterfowl, who I have had the pleasure of sharing a blind with, both for geese and ducks. They deploy an array of the finest decoys made, and on a nice dry day Ben will even use real mounted Canada's for the spread. It's hard to beat that. Being a taxidermist myself, it has always been a goal of mine to run stuffers. It is just something I have never got around to doing. I also do not have the space to store and travel with them. Ben has an entire trailer dedicated to his. Now that is hardcore. If those boys heard me announce myself as a hardcore goose guy they would get quite a chuckle.
    I have to admit that the pounding power of goose wings whistling and hovering yards over my head is a rush that not much can match. I just can't dedicate the time to be considered hardcore. I am a prisoner to the need

for variety in the wings I chase. For me, this means most of my time in the field chasing Canada's has mixed, even humorous results. To do it right, or to guide for a living, you simply have to invest countless hours and many miles scouting. These are hours and miles that I have chosen to spend elsewhere.

In our early years, Jason and I spent quite a bit of time in the Connell area, just south of Othello, where we had some fields locked up. We had enough real estate secured to come over the pass and spend a day or two to find geese, but as any good goose hunter knows you need more than just a few fields. We have had days where we thought we would make Ben proud, and of course some days we were hoping no one was watching!

The early goose season in Washington provided us time to do a little August scouting when nothing was going on, and even better, shoot waterfowl in September, which also has no conflicts. For years the only place available was the southern portion of the state, everything south of HWY 3 that runs parallel with the Columbia River, from I-5 to the rivers mouth by Ilwaco. We spent a lot of time in the Cathalamet area to the little river town of Altoona. This lasted until 1997 when the regulations changed, now you can hunt the entire state. The early season dates change every year but tend to last about a week. What was special about the hunts down south was the chance at the elusive Dusky Canada Goose. They usually do not arrive until well into November but there were always a few stragglers mixed in with the flocks. They became a main goal on those hunts, one that took us three years to finally accomplish. Had we shot them during the regular season in that area we would have lost our permit and not been allowed back in the region. Once there are too many Dusky's shot, they close the season all together making those that target this dark little goose not too popular. We looked at it as another good reason to use the September season for this goal. As taxidermists know though, it does present a slight problem. Canada's are in molt this time of year making it rather difficult to mount. Nothing like a good challenge we figured, and I still have the Dusky on my wall.

Driving back from the Dove hunt we started mulling over our goose plans. Jason was watching a small flock that had been running the slough not too far from Marysville where we lived, although he doubted he would even be able to join us. I did a few scouting runs closer to the Cascade foothills in the Granite Falls area but had come up pretty much empty. Captain Dave had the best option. He had noticed a rather large flock of Greaters working a small inlet bay in south Hood Canal. I had never hunted in the Hood Canal before and this sounded like a good adventure. Jason eventually chose to stay home, and with his blessing we chose the Canal. He couldn't leave the golf course long enough, what with all the September hot weather, to make the trip to the Peninsula. Or any place for that matter. We dropped him off and then swung by my house for some fresh clothes. I had just enough time to kiss the wife and kids, and was once again on the road. No rest for the wicked.

I love the rust that builds on a hunter from an off-season. The little things that come automatically while in full swing are often forgotten early on. Even after years of experience, those early season hunts are nothing more than practice. We arrived the next morning at the spot where we were to put the Aqua Pods in the water, only to notice the tide was too low. Two seasoned Sea Duckers hunting on the salt, and neither of us bothered to check the tides. This detail would haunt us the entire day. After a long hike down to a small cliff on the muddy shoreline, and another hike with our small boats and tons of gear, we arrived to where we were supposed to find water.

A funny detail about early season hunts is that you acquire all this new gear in the summer, which we all know needs to be used. We were prepared for 30 degrees below with enough gear to last a month if we were stranded. I think I even had some tags I forgot to take off on one of my shirts. Of course the low temperature for the day was 60 degrees and the hunt was planned for about two or three hours. Captain Dave makes over packing an art form. Being a total gear nut he just has to bring it all. When we finally reached the water we discovered it was about three inches deep, with about a half mile to paddle. Have I mentioned yet that I am a part time goose guy?

After struggling for what seemed an eternity in those three inches and working up quite a nice sweat, we finally came to a point where we could use our paddles. It was sheer heaven to be gliding freely in the open water. Dave brought Marley, his aged but trusty Chesapeake, and she would swim along side us all the way to our spot. Marley has a way of drinking and swimming at the same time that comes in handy. I just follow the yaps as we zigzagged through seemingly endless little canals that were unfamiliar to me in the dark. I saw Dave coast to shore and noticed a tide pool about thirty yards over from the spit he landed on. We had arrived.

"Hey Johnny Boy, you set your blind there, I'll set mine here and let's get these dekes out . . ." Dave whispered with a smile while walking down the sandy beach. I always pay attention when he calls me that, I know that means he is as giddy as a school girl. Hunt with a guy long enough and you learn the little things and hints that tell you where your partners are at mentally. Had he just pointed I would have known to turn back.

I reached into my bag of dekes to find an absolute mess. I have one Carry Light Brant floater that I always set in my Canada spread, and wouldn't you know it the cord had come unraveled and tangled with all the others. Cheap decoy anyway, I just couldn't bear to let it go. Jason and I had it float into our spread one day on a tide rip in Samish Bay while hunting Oldsquaws and we have used it for our anchor float for years. We figured it brought good luck and always made sure we had it whenever we hunted any kind of geese, some luck so far!

After untangling the mess I managed to deploy all my other floaters. I used my decoys on the north side of the spread in front of my blind and Dave set the south. We tried to make the middle as a sort of landing zone but we really got a good laugh once the sun started to peek out and we saw all our handy work. Next for me came my G&H shells. These are about twenty years old and have to be handled quite delicately, the sun has really done a number throughout the years. The ground was nice and soft, no new cracks on this hunt. Lastly I put out my silhouettes. These were very special to Jason and me, we made them ourselves. Jason is quite a good sketch artist and hand drew our pattern. After that we made cut outs on plywood, painted them up, and put on steel spikes for those frozen ground days. This made these bad boys extremely heavy and the most we could ever use were the dozen we made. Being pretty passionate about trying to be as traditional as possible, I will not hunt geese without at least a couple out. Put together we had about eight dozen in the water and on the beach, not too bad. The goose guys could appreciate our numbers but I can mentally picture Ben shaking his head at the quality, and I don't blame him. Maybe someday an upgrade is in order. Those Dave Smiths are pretty sweet.

The sky was a bit overcast, prolonging our darkness. This was the least of our problems. The closest decoys in the water were already on the shore. Wouldn't you know it but our tide was still leaving. Not knowing the area or the tide I had no idea how long we would have our water. All I could think about as I peered over the blind was I sure hoped the geese came, and what a pain it would be to move all these decoys.

When I first heard them I was almost in disbelief. The distant honking had me realizing I was actually there, and tingles shot down my legs. Here comes the first flock, right when Dave said they would, about a half hour after sunrise. One of the best attributes of a September goose is their lack of knowledge, and these did not disappoint. In they came; in their minds this was no different than any other morning. As I gave a quick blow on my call, they gave a quick shake. Oh man, that was terrible. I heard Dave chuckle at my attempt, and that call was in the sand. At this point, all I could do was mess it up anyway. The flock was 30 strong and locked onto our decoys. I waited to hear Dave give the call . . . I figured his place, his deal. I did a quick look to make sure I was loaded. I had already made so many errors that I didn't trust myself.

"Wait . . . . wait . . ." Dave was showing unusual patience. His nickname is Slappy Jack for many reasons, and I am not just talking about his willingness to go all in at the sight of a one-eyed Jack the moment it is dealt to him. I could feel myself start to shake when I heard the humming of the large wings. The flock had split in two sections, one on my side and one on his. They had no idea what was about to happen and our sloppy old rig was working like a charm. There were no circling, they came straight in. I peeked over to Dave, my patience running low. He cocked his head, waited, and then yelled "NOW!"

I pulled up to find a pair within ten yards. I took two shots, and two huge Greaters fell into the water. I was so excited that not only did I not hear Dave shoot, but I lost the rest of the flock, and didn't even bother trying to shoot another. I saw Marley scream into the water and she began to chase one I didn't quite kill cleanly. In seconds she was bringing it back to me. I scanned the water quickly to see how Dave had done to find he had tripled. His three clean kills lay right out before him. All were within fifteen yards of his blind. I jumped out of the blind and met him at the edge, where he was already standing, directing Marley on the rest. Lots of high fives, even shared an excited hug or two. The rust was officially off for Waterfowl. The season can now begin.

We quickly got organized and sat back in the blind. Our water now was almost gone. At this point I was happy and moving was out of the question. The limit is four Canada's and we only needed three more, but I was content to end right there. I called Marly over to the blind for some proper ear scratching of thanks as I admired the birds lying next to me in the sand.

About an hour later, with essentially no water at all, we started getting restless. This was new territory for me so I stood up to take a look around. That is when I saw them coming. The tide was very low that day and people were beginning to walk in to harvest the oysters that were exposed. I couldn't believe it, oysters were everywhere. A fellow then came out of nowhere and gave us the look like "what the heck are you doing". Dave gave me the old smirk of lets get out of here, mission accomplished.

The walk back was even more grueling than the walk in. Our water canals now looked like hiker trails, filled with the hoards of oyster shuckers. The funny looks we got were priceless. Most folks are not aware such an early hunting season exists. Not to be left out, we managed to harvest a few oysters ourselves while we hiked. Nothing like fresh cooked half shells and barbequed goose breasts to complete the day.

Later that afternoon our hopes were dashed for tomorrow's hunt after we checked the tides for next day. They were even lower than before. Frankly I was tired. I felt lucky enough to get one day of September Canada hunting in and was completely satisfied. We only got the one flock, but as they say, it's not how many flocks you decoy, it's what you do with those flocks. I still had to drive home and that involves the good old Washington State ferry system, and at this point I was really missing my family. After six straight days of chasing Doves and Geese, it was sure going to feel good to sleep in my own bed.

Chapter 4

Band-Tail Pigeons

I was getting soaked. The amount of dew that falls off of the branches of trees at over 4,000 feet above sea level is almost as equal to taking a shower as you brush against the lush needles. I had made a little cubby of space amongst the wild huckleberries and the ferns and was trying to hide myself using the fallen cedar branches. I think the blind in this situation was more for me as the area was so thick with cover I could have worn a neon orange suit and not be seen. The birds would be coming from the bottom of a valley, swooping up to the ridge where we were nestled. We were miles from any type of civilization, miles from any artificial lights or noise. It was dark, about twenty minutes before sunrise, and I could still barely see ten feet in front of me. It was the land of the Band-Tail Pigeon, a bird held in the highest regard to us Otto boys, our favorite hunt of the year.

As I was putting on the finishing touches to the blind, I heard it. The loudest snort I have ever experienced, so close I actually felt it in my chest. The eerie silence right after had me frozen. Before I could think, I heard the beast crashing down into the valley. I had set up maybe ten yards from where a big Cascade Mountain Black Bear was about to settle down for the day. After I composed myself I was grateful for the little reminder. We were not in our house, but his. This land belongs to the bears, the elk, and the deer. I had better be prepared. I had been here many times before, seen all the bear "signs", and knew that the huckleberries that were drawing in the Band-Tail Pigeons were also a favorite to the bears and other wildlife. Still, it is not often a somewhat city boy like me finds myself in such a wild place while it is pitch black.

After I finished up my blind, I walked over to Jason to see his spot. He likes to line up at the edge of the old growth timbers that feed down into the valley. This stretch of old growth is maybe 500 yards deep and creates another edge on the opposite side before coming to an end with a huge rocky cliff. On both sides were clear cuts from about fifteen years ago, long enough to where the trees and cover were starting to get rather high. We access the area, about twenty miles north of Concrete, from an old logging road. It is a rough one that is barely drivable. Once on top of the ridge, we parked and hiked the rest. There is about a half mile of trail that the Band-Tails like to fly through from feeding to resting. At over 4,000 feet up our view was breathtaking. To the southwest you can actually see the skyscrapers of downtown Seattle. Barely peaking over a foothill, they seem so small and insignificant from our vantage point. In all other directions you can see miles of mountain tops and rolling forests. My mind drifts again and I think to myself this is what the Northwest looked like before white man carved civilization into this once vastly forested corner of earth. I feel lucky to see such splendor.

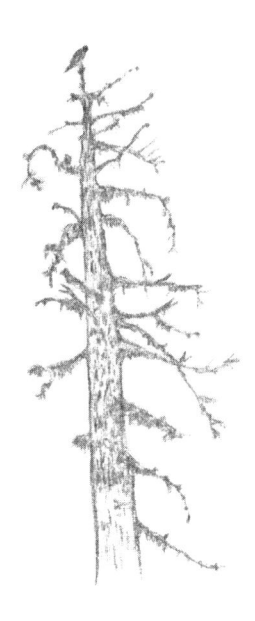

Joining us on the ridge were our good friends Kasey Cummings and Chris Engelhardt. These two are cousins and are as close as friends as Jason and I.

Both have never hunted Band-Tails but are experienced Waterfowl hunters in their own right. Chris is a very deep insightful type of guy, spending the day in the blind with him is a great reminder of the importance of reflecting and cherishing the days spent a field. He always has a way of making every moment special, everything means something.

The romantic way I would talk of Band-Tails had him chomping at the bit to hit the hills, and I was really excited to be there for his first harvest. Kasey on the other hand is the polar opposite on the exterior. He calls a spade a spade and has a rather rough demeanor, but the more you get to know him the more you realize why he and Chris are so close. The gruffness is just a façade; they are two peas in a pod. I have always said that I don't "love" hunting, I "feel" it. I am part of it. Of course this usually gets a chuckle from most, but not these two. They understand. These are the kind of guys I love to hunt with.

Two more people were also with us. This year Jason and I wanted to really share the experience of Band-Tails. The limit is only two birds a day, and the season is a mere seven days long. With the numbers of Pigeons in our spot, we could afford the luxury of sharing. A spread out group hunt seemed appropriate. Pat White, or "Paddy" as he likes to be called, also accepted our invitation. Paddy is a dyed in the wool Quail hunter who on occasion loves to go Waterfowl hunting. He is on a quest to harvest all the game birds of North America, much like myself, and for certain wouldn't miss the chance to get the elusive Band-Tail. When Paddy told me he had been practicing at the range for this I could not help but smile. I knew they haven't invented a way to simulate their flight patterns and that later Paddy would come to find this out.

Rounding out our group was Ben Welton. Ben is a longtime friend, and a long time wing chaser. Now in his sixties, Ben has led a life dedicated to hunting and conservation. The first bird Ben harvested as a young man was a Band-Tail Pigeon. To say this hunt was special for him was an understatement. Health issues had kept him away. His old haunts are filled with deep ravines and long hikes. Here we were able to drive him close to where he needed to be. He chose to hunt the farthest point out, next to the cliffs and the roughest terrain. I think he did this on purpose, not for our sake, but for him. I could tell he wanted to work harder than us; it is just the way he is. He also wasn't content on setting up near the trail. He had to climb up in the rough cover for what he called a "better view". I hope I have the drive he has when I reach that age, and have accomplished half as much.

After I left Jason I walked down to check on Paddy, who was set up on the opposite old growth line. Chris and Kasey were at the beginning of the trail, set up together. The plan was to slowly group together as we all limited. This way we could share each others experiences and also help find downed birds. One problem hunting here in such wild, thick cover is locating birds. Losing one is not an option. We had a team of dogs on duty for the hunt. Kasey brought his chocolate lab aptly named CoCo. She is a fine dog, getting up there in years, but has lots of talent. Jason of course had Ruddy, but using her up here was a challenge itself. She is barely two years old and completely deaf, so he has to be careful where and when to send her. The dogs will be instantly out of sight and must be highly whistle trained. I was lucky enough to have Teal. Her small size allowed her to twist and turn in the smallest of openings. Ben brought his dog Deke, a fine little Boykin with little experience. He kept her close to his side. Paddy also had his pointer, a German Wirehair named Eli. This gave us quite a motley crew of pups, and I enjoy that. Having only been around Labs my entire life it was good to see other breeds in action.

Climbing back into my blind I could see the sun was starting to peek through a distant mountain top. There was still a haze of fog that was drifting through the valley making the visibility that much more challenging. It was still and quiet. I looked down at Jason, who was on my right about twenty yards away. I could see he was working hard to peer into the growing light. I couldn't see the others but I knew Jason was in the best spot. We set it up that way so he would be able to photograph the rest of the day. Being a part time professional photographer has him thinking of pictures now more than meat. But pictures would come later. Band-Tails are a first light mover. When the flights are strong, they can last for a couple of hours. If they are weak, maybe only twenty minutes. It was critical time.

I could only hear the first flock that flew over me. It had to have been twenty strong, their wings clicking as they scurried by. That tell tale sound stirred the butterflies in me, here they come. The next flight I picked up a bit early. As they lifted up the hillside towards me they erratically change flight and headed straight to where Chris and Kasey are. Seconds later I heard the first shot. CoCo was crashing into the cover. I would later learn that Kasey had missed. The excitement of the moment got to him. Their first encounter with the Band-Tail taught them a thing or two. These birds are big and they cut faster than a Dove, and have the moves of Teal on steroids.

His shot rustled a few more flocks that were roosted down below. The next flock coming had too many birds to count. It looked like thousands but was more likely to be around a hundred. They roared up over Jason and me, chaos darting everywhere. They were simply too close together, too close for a shot. You have to be responsible with a two bird limit, no room for error. Only perfect shots are allowed. A long shot can send a bird over a cliff or down a long ravine making it irretrievable. I quickly glanced over to see that Jason was already looking my way with a big smile on his face. I don't think we had ever seen that many at one time, and with not a shot to be had.

Still looking over his way I saw a trio that were following the crowd. They worked a perfect line right up the old growth. I watched as the whole event unfolded. At about twenty yards high they floated over Jason's head and he slowly raised his gun. Bang! A clean shot! Bang! Another wing folded, it was perfection. A finer display of composure had surely never been witnessed. One bird fell onto the trail where Ruddy quickly picked it up. He called her back and motioned for me to bring Teal for the other. I walked over and sent her in. Moments later, out she came, bird in mouth. Just like that Jason was done. He was overwhelmed, his arms were shaking, and all he could do was sit. I handed him his quarry and sat beside him. I put my arm around his shoulder and didn't say a word. We just took it all in. I looked around at the peaceful place we had just interrupted; it seemed rude to make any more sounds. All was said.

Our moment came to an end when an excited Chris came running around the corner to greet us.

"I heard shots, how'd you do?" He whispered. It was strange, nothing was ever mentioned about being quiet, the place just had that affect on every one.

"Sit down, let me show you . . ." Jason finally said. His voice was a bit cracked and he never lifted his eyes off his birds. He knew how much Chris had simply anticipated holding one let alone harvesting his own. Jason handed one over, both treated it like porcelain. Chris immediately got out a pencil and tablet and started sketching.

"Where is Kasey?" I asked as they studied.

"He can't move, didn't you hear the bear? This is all too much for him." I would later learn they thought they spooked the bear. Kasey loves to hunt bruins and pledged to return soon to see him face to face. The snort and overall noise created had everyone thinking he was close to them.

"Chris, stay with Jason, I'll keep Kasey company."

I brought Teal to heel and headed back. I didn't get ten yards when I heard the twigs on the trail break with a scurry. I turned around to see another flock ascending the hill. I took a knee and waited. They seemed to wise up a bit and began to dance just out of range. A lone bird broke free and headed straight at me. I pulled up and gave it a shot. My first shot startled even me, the nerves hit hard. My second rang true and he folded a little far down the ravine. I sent Teal who made it a quick retrieve. I held my first bird in hand. It was a little wet from the trip through the brush, and considering it was a juvenile it didn't have too many feathers to spare. In my excitement I didn't even hear Chris shoot. Ruddy was just coming out with a bird in her mouth, we had doubled. I quickly paced back to the boys.

I had never seen such a look of accomplishment on anyone's face as I did on Chris. This harvest was a culmination of months of studying up on the bird, reading everything he could get his hands on. Now that he had achieved his goal, it was time for a victory smoke. We laid out our birds so we could admire them and I reached in my shooters vest for some of Puerto Rico's finest. We had a few birds flying around us but we didn't care. Moments later Kasey came around the bend. He had heard the shooting and figured it was time to join the group.

In hand the Band-Tail is magnificent. The first thing that jumps out at you is the yellow beak and feet, striking colors when played off the overall gray appearance. The chest and top of the head of the most mature birds have a pinkish hue. The eyes are dark brown surrounded by ringlets of red. On the back of the neck is the tell tale horizontal white stripe, one of the last marks of plumage to mature. Underneath the stripe are the green feathers that resemble scales that flow into its back. The wingtips are black, as well as the stripe that cuts across the tail feathers giving them their name.

The flight continued strong well into the morning. The four of us quickly finished up our limits and Jason was reeling off pictures left and right. I was able to take a perfect specimen, one I could save for taxidermy. After that

I decided to hike to the other side of the old growth to see how Paddy and Ben were doing. When I got there I was met with some wide eyes.

"Have you seen all those Band-Tails?" Paddy was still in shock. I could see a nicely plumed bird sitting on the stump he was leaning on.

"We still have them flying all over; we have been done for a while. How are you guys fairing?" I answered.

"I've got one, but should have been done an hour ago, Ben hasn't even shot. So much for the practice at the range!"

I sent Paddy to join the others and proceeded to climb the hill into the scrub to join Ben. I was greeted with a large smile and an invitation to join him among the huckleberries. Band-Tails were literally all over us.

"Here comes one Ben, to the left!" I excitedly whispered. The bird floated on by, Ben didn't even raise his gun.

"Not the right one." As he said this as he looked directly at me. His face seemed quite serious. I had hunted ducks and geese with Ben, but never Pigeons. On those hunts Ben was famous for being very selective in what he shot, nothing too different than anyone in my camp. Here it is impossible to tell male from female, and I wasn't sure if it was an issue of plumage or what he was waiting on.

"Which one are you looking for?" I asked.

"I'll know."

We sat together on that hill for over two hours. I do not exaggerate when I say Ben had at least forty different shots, and for Band-Tails that is a huge amount. The conversation drifted from his youth, to the upcoming season, and to what the Band-Tail had meant to him. I was starting to wonder if he was ever going to shoot. Periodically Jason would come up from below and ask if everything was alright. Paddy had picked up his last bird and the rest of the crew was content to let us sit up there all day if need be.

At about as non-descript of a moment as I could describe, a Pigeon came swooping up from the lower left hand side. This was something birds had been doing all day long, but this one must have been different. Suddenly, out of the corner of my eye, I saw movement. Ben was getting ready. The Band-Tail hovered out in front of us, almost as if it wanted to land on the very stump Ben was sitting on. He pulled up and squeezed the trigger. The noise actually startled me. I knew it was coming, but the fact he shot was still came as a bit of a surprise. The bird folded ten yards below him. Deke was sent into action and within a minute had the bird back to his hand. Ben just stared down at the bird, moving his fingers through the feathers, and petting Deke with his free hand. I quickly pulled out my little digital camera and caught the moment.

"Only one more to go, Ben."

"Nope, I'm done. Let's go." He said without even looking up.
"Was that the 'one'?"
"Yes, John, that was the one. Someday you will understand."

I sat and reflected on that as he gathered his gear. What did he mean I will someday understand? I felt like I did. I still feel like I do. But I have a lot of living to do before I get to where he is in life. When I arrive there maybe I will see more than the obvious meanings. Perhaps, sometimes, only the reflection on a total life lived can help you understand. I hope to be that fortunate.

We left the mountain elated. Days like this come along rarely, if at all. In my many years of watching the Band-Tail, I had never seen that many. Even Ben was hard pressed to remember such numbers. Given their tumultuous past, it had been exciting to see. We returned three more times in the seven day season. Jason and I got limits all three times but the amount of birds were dividing in half with each passing day until the final day they were all but gone. We select only guests who had the utmost respect for the Band-Tail. All too often some hunters regard them as just a "park pigeon" giving them no more respect than the birds found eating garbage at the dump. That is considering they have even heard of them. One guest we did invite was a fellow by the name of Dan Drust who represented Filson Clothing. We met while working on a partnership that had been created with Filson and our Washington Brant Foundation. One of his life goals was to simply see one. Coming from the East Coast, he felt it was his best chance at seeing the bird that is closest relative to the historic Passenger Pigeon. I watched as he waited patiently for over four hours just for his first sighting, and then another two before he was lucky enough to harvest one. This is the kind of respect that should be bestowed upon one of the most majestic creatures that inhabits our forests.

Chapter 5

Waterfowl Opening Day Weekend

Opening weekend is my Christmas, Birthday, and Thanksgiving, all rolled into one action packed event. It is high tradition for my brother and me to go all out, spare no expense. If by Monday we don't need extra sleep, we didn't do something right. The local puddle ducks are usually fairly uneducated and plentiful, with the newly arrived sea ducks all colored up and fresh to our waters. Spirits are always high. The optimism for the season ahead has me charged and ready to go. I simply can't wait.

On Friday night, or, "Opening Day Eve" as we rather tongue in cheek refer to it, we host a big barbeque and invite as many of our Waterfowling friends that can make it. Most guys are busy packing for trips or have even already gone, but we do get a crowd of ten or so, all excited as we are and ready to celebrate. This year it was decided to have it at my house. Captain

Dave had arrived early in the morning so we could get all our gear ready to go. The others were set to join us around seven.

"So Dave, what is your goal this year?" I asked as we began loading up our boat. I think I asked this of everyone eventually that night. I am of the opinion that every year a Waterfowler should enter the season with some sort of goal. I think this helps us to focus and can really get the juices going. It is really fulfilling when you achieve goals that you may have thought were difficult, if not impossible. I set quite a few every year for myself.

"Simple, Dave replied, to get in as much action as possible before the clients show up!" He sure answered that fast!

A couple of hours later Jason arrived at my house, and we put the finishing touches on the gear. Our plan is simple, and it hasn't changed in ten years. On the Saturday morning opener, we set up for puddle ducks, and only shoot three apiece. Where tradition really sets in is when we hit the salts for Scoters, mainly Surfs. The limit for those is four, so by limiting ourselves to three puddle ducks we do two things. One, we leave enough limit for the Scoters, and two, we extend a day that at most times can be over quite quickly. After the salt hunt we will take a ferry over to Captain Dave's neck of the woods for our annual Harlequin duck hunt the next morning. We used to do both hunts on our side, but changed that so we could really stretch out the terrain and quite frankly, hit a healthier population of Harlequins. For every Harly we see in our haunts, there are five or six on his side. Considering how geographically habitual Harlequins tend to stay, it just made sense to hunt his river systems. Harlequins have a "one per season" limit so this hunt is quite special and very unique. We three were part of a small group of concerned Waterfowlers that helped initiate that process and the seasonal limit in order to protect and preserve gunning for the little blue duck for many years to come. Better to be able to harvest one a year than none at all. After that hunt we finish out Sunday setting up again for Scoters, only this time we try and focus on White-Wings.

"Hey, where do we put the beer?" I could hear Don Spidell shout out as he headed up the driveway. Don is a fellow sea duck hunter, and more importantly, an accomplished decoy carver. I say important because you always want to keep your carving friends happy, if you know what I mean.

"In the garage fridge with all the others, it's good to see you!" I rushed out to shake his hand and saw that he was carrying a box. "What you got there?"

"Nothing, nothing at all. Just give me a cold one and fire up that barbeque," he said with a coy little smile.

For dinner everyone always brings something neat for the grill and this year was no exception. For my portion I had prepared Texas Dove from the birds left over from our earlier trip. Dove ranks up there with filet mignon with this crowd. Dave brought some Canvasback meat from the year prior and was planning a stir fry with a little garlic and wine, one of my favorites. Jason's addition was Band-Tail pigeon poppers. This was going to be a big hit, not everyone who was coming had the pleasure of tasting Band-Tail, and they were in for a treat. Don handed me a big bag of deer jerky which I promptly put on a tray for some easy snacking.

"I heard there were some bums giving out free food? Have I got the right place?" Immediately I knew Chris and Kasey had arrived. Kasey has one of those voices that can cut right through a crowd and commands attention.

"No, you've come to the PETA rally; please check all leather and furs at the door sir!" My impromptu joke got a few chuckles as I embraced my fellow brothers at the edge of my garage. Chris was also carrying a box, which had to be good. He is another one of those carver guys.

"So, what are you cooking?" I asked Chris. He is like Dave, and he takes barbequing quite seriously. A few years back we had a big carver's day workshop, hosted by Captain Dave, where Chris made us all a brisket that took the entire day to cook. It was unbelievable. Watching him work on that piece of meat was like watching an artist create magic on canvas.

"Grouse steaks. I also plan on backing you up, just in case, of course," he said, with a funny gleam in his eye. I knew exactly what he meant. It didn't matter what I was cooking, he always takes over. Don't get me wrong, I actually love it. I am a hack with a spatula, and a master like him just doesn't have the patience to watch me turn those Doves. What he doesn't know is that's all part of my plan. Turning over the grill just gets me out of that responsibility.

"Does anyone here like Quail?" Paddy White strolled right in the garage holding a Tupperware container that held thirty of the nicest little white meat breasts, all in a dark marinade. Paddy loved hunting quail, and the season had been open for the week leading up to this. He had hunted the first four days with excellent success, which meant good grub for our little event.

When the core group of guys that we had invited got there, Jason and I assembled them into the garage. It was time for our unofficial opening ceremony and I wanted to say a few things before a few other casual friends and guests showed up. The group here was sort of the center of our hunting crew, maybe missing a couple here and there. We had a few surprises for our guests and I wanted to put them into a good mood before the beer and food took over. This was our little way of getting the season started off on the right foot.

After I thanked them all for coming and talked a little duck, I gave a few words of encouragement for the upcoming year. I then had them all stand in a line and close their eyes. Jason set a decoy at each of their feet.

"O.K. guys, you can open your eyes. If you would look down you will see a gift we want all of you to have. The only promise you make to us is that you float these at least once this year," I said as I walked over to stand by Jason. We gave them each a Scoter decoy that came out of our rig from years earlier. They were the first decoys we had carved, and they had seen a lot of waves. They weren't going to win any contests on land, but in the water these proved deadly. We called them our "old school rig", coming from our original three dozen. Most were retired, as these were, and we thought it would be cool to get some of those back out on the water. Drewry's decoy was a Black Scoter and this gave him all of the three species out of our old rig, something he had been wanting.

"Oh guys, that is way cool, can't thank you enough." Chris said staring down at his decoy. "Now you two have to open that box over there."

Jason walked over and cracked open the box. Inside was a beautiful solid cedar Red Breasted Merganser he carved and signed for our rig. We didn't expect that.

"Thanks guys, this means a lot to me," Don piped in, "now you have to open my box."

I opened his to find a stunning cork Surf Scoter decoy that also came out of his personal rig. I knew this was special, as it was also one of his firsts.

"O.K., my turn!" Drewry turned back to his truck and came back with a box of his own. Inside was a solid cedar Black Scoter decoy for our rig.

The next few minutes were spent by all of us admiring our new decoys and taking in everyone's generosity. We all couldn't believe that such a decoy swap had just happened without any planning. On the spot we quickly decided that the decoys would be used over the weekend and signed them to commemorate the event.

"Now that you guys are all done singing Kum-By-Yah, can a guy get a beer and some meat around here, sheesh!" We all laughed, Kasey always had a way with words and his timing was appropriate. If he hadn't intervened, we would have started talking about our "feelings" or something, which is a serious guy code violation. Deep down though, I couldn't help but think of how lucky I was to have friends like this. We all punched each other in the shoulders and cracked some fresh beers.

The grilling, eating and overall festivities lasted well into the evening. There is something about the conversation that transpires when you put a bunch of hunters together. The "you should have been there's", and the "I can't believe I saw's", plus of course we basically solved all the problems we face as sportsmen. It was the same dialogue that takes place wherever two or more hunters have gathered. When all the meat was displayed on the table it was an unbelievable sight. A finer feast had never been witnessed.

My wife Toni had cooked up all the trimmings including her famous cheesy potatoes which are always a big hit. She also baked a big cake that celebrated the start of the season, complete with a frosted Mallard of her own creation. We all ate too much and most certainly had too much fun. We were off to a great start.

Most of the guys stayed the night and headed out to their morning destinations from my house. Chris and Kasey always took Kasey's father-in-law to their lease, which they called the "Doctors Property" in the Snohomish River valley. After their hunt they will join up with us at Dave's place for the Harlequin hunt Sunday morning. Don went puddle duck hunting on his favorite lake with his long time hunting partner. Paddy always meets up with Ben Welton for the opener for Bluebills on Padilla Bay. Ben had done this in one form or another for years. He would have joined us in our get together, but he wanted to get on the water at around two in the morning, much too early to even think about doing something the night before.

In the morning we set out to the beach that would host the first leg of our weekend hunts. The beach is on a brackish lake that is created by the high tide of the nearby Skagit bay. It is a small walk of about two hundred yards from the truck to the blind. We picked this spot because we knew that if we went much further we would have to hear Dave complain about how we should be in a boat. Walking is so uncivilized to the hardened diver hunter. To be honest, I couldn't agree more. I've been on a couple of marathon hikes with Dave, or as he calls them, "death marches," and we generally try to stay away from them. Boy I am getting lazy in my old age.

I opened the truck door and stepped out. It was unbelievably warm. This meant a sweaty day in the chest waders. I appreciated not having the bone chilling cold that was too come in a month or so, but the warmth would make the hunt hard on different levels. I probably wouldn't do well living in Florida. There are worse problems, I thought as I put on my head lamp. It was also very dark, there being no street lights where we parked. This I enjoy, it makes me feel a little more out in the wild. Living in Western Washington we do not get to experience this very much near the salt water. There is always that element of fear that someone is going to rush out of the bushes, and if they were, they would certainly be up to no good. Silly thoughts, but it does get a bit creepy in the dark at some of the places Waterfowling takes you. I again thought about Florida, at least there are no alligators in the streams I am about to cross.

"Looks like the blind needs a little work, I will take care of that, you guys get those decoys out. We have about fifteen minutes to opening gun and I want to be ready." Captain Dave began to take charge. We have dubbed ourselves the "three captains", three guys ready and willing to take the bull by the horns, all generals and no soldiers. Mostly the first person to start barking out orders takes lead and this morning, Dave was that man. As soon as we threw out the last decoy he walked over and inspected our work. He immediately waded out and moved about a third of our two dozen dekes. If he had done nothing I would have been concerned. We just smiled and started organizing our gear in the blind.

The five minutes before firing time on opening day have got to be the longest five minutes known to man. The sounds of the marsh were everywhere. I could hear the constant calling of the hen Mallard down the way, and the sound of the ducks winging unseen over the decoys. I can literally feel my pulse in my arms. I try to get a fix on the birds as they swing through the rig, but the darkness reduces them to blurs. The sky was a bit overcast, meaning the dark conditions would hold on a bit longer. I could see some movement on the water; ducks had begun to land and were swimming about.

"It's time," Jason whispered, "the duck season is now open!"

Peering through the flocks, I could make out more now. There were Wigeon, Teal, Mallards, and Shoveler. We wanted three birds apiece, and I didn't really care what kind they were. I prefer Teal but I won't be picky. The plan was to barbeque these birds for dinner. Teal are my favorite puddle duck to eat, but I do love them all.

I looked down at my watch, about ten minutes had passed. There were lots of shots to be had. I still was having a hard time telling drake from hen. Most puddle ducks were still in eclipse plumage making it harder in the low light. Several birds were coming in over my left shoulder, and since I was on the far left side, I decided to turn around to see them better. This was good also in the sense there was better light in that direction. A few hen Wigeon passed before a nice pair of Mallards came hovering over. I could now easily see which one was the drake. He was above the hen as they came descending down, right at me. I raised my gun and let out a shot. The drake fell into the sand, dead on impact. This caused quite an uproar; all the birds that were swimming inside our decoys lifted and joined the already fleeing flocks. Dave let out one shot on the departing birds and dropped a single drake Wigeon. We both quickly left the blind to grab our birds and met up at the edge of the water.

"Nice shot John, how did that feel?"

"Oh man, that was nice. Let me see your Wigeon," I replied and held out my hand to hold his bird. His drake was a first year bird lacking the white shoulder patch Wigeon get in their second year. While having both birds in hand I noticed my Mallard was feather perfect. He looked like a nice December hog, an obvious old mature drake. His curls were full and dark green. I handed the Wigeon back to Dave and nestled back down in the blind. I couldn't take my eyes off my Mallard. The first place I check on a drake such as this is the gray feathers of his side pockets. Sure enough, this bird had the white tips, one of the last of the feathers to come into plume. How fortunate I was to be able to start off with such a fine bird. Not only that, I am a little superstitious. I was once told that if the first bird of the season matches the last bird taken the season prior, you would have good luck. My last bird last year was a nice Mallard taken over Scoter decoys. I felt good about that.

"Hey Dave, what was your last bird you shot last year?" I just had to ask.

"Uh, let me think. Oh yeah, it was a nice drake Surf Scoter. You were there, why do you ask?"

"No reason . . ."

After a bit of a lull, a flock of Teal came screaming past the decoys. They took one swoop and committed as early season birds tend to do. Jason pulled up and doubled on two really nice drake Green Wings, dropping them both in the middle of the rig. As the flock left I noticed one bird seemed out of place. The wings were much brighter, this bird stuck out like a sore thumb. I knew what that meant. I pulled up, and dropped it as they tried to speed around the corner of where we were set up. I wasted no time running to the edge and waded out to get it. I was right, a nice Cinnamon Teal. It was a first year hen, and I knew I was going to get it from the guys for shooting her, but I didn't care. I enjoy shooting Cinnamon and Blue Wing Teal early season, just about the only time we see them. Normally these birds would already be down to Oregon by now. Seems my luck had already started.

The next twenty minutes were filled with flock after flock trying to pound into our little hole. My third bird was another Teal, this time a nice little young Green Wing drake. Jason got another Green Wing while Dave shot a nice double on Wigeon. We had our three apiece and it was time to move on. Some years it takes longer, some years the action can be so furious we don't want to leave. This year it was just right. The hunt had lasted about an hour and a half, perfect timing to still catch the morning flights of Surfs. We had four different species and were quite happy with that. We picked up the dekes in short order, and hiked out.

The drive to the launch was about a half hour away and we wanted to waste no time. When we arrived we started doing the mad shuffle to get our boat ready to launch. We run a 16 foot Alaskan Smoker Craft with a deep "V" hull powered by a 25 horse Honda 4 Stroke that we bought from Chris Engelhardt at Valley RV & Marine in Mount Vernon. We chose this boat, with the help of Chris's expert opinion, for its safety and versatility. It comfortably hunts three in the open water with plenty of room left over for gear and a dog. In no time flat we were on the salt and headed to our spot.

I sat in the bow of the boat and was on log watching duty. It felt good to feel the wind and the sea spray hitting my face as we bounced along. There was a mild chop in the water, but the seas were relatively calm, perfect for a nice early season sea duck hunt.

Once we got to our destination we worked as a team deploying the long lines and setting the decoys. Jason and I have done this so many times we could do it in our sleep. Normally adding a person to this task slows it down, but not with Dave. Even though he may do it slightly different, this is also second nature to him. He fits right in. With his help we were down and ready to hunt in minutes.

The rig today was about four dozen strong, all cork and cedar. Besides the decoys we had received the night before, this particular rig is made up of several carvers that we have collected throughout the years. A couple dekes that immediately come to mind are from a carver well known for hunting Scoters on the east coast in Chesapeake Bay, Jeff Coats. He carved two Black Scoters that he donated to our Washington Brant Foundation that both Jason and I had to have. We purchased them in our live auction after running them on the salt for a year per Jeff's request. My favorite, though, has to be a trio that Jason himself carved.

Most of our decoys in this rig came from my brother, but these three are special. Representing the Brant Foundation he flew to Maryland and entered the famed decoy contest put on by the Ward Foundation, the World Championships. The competition is broke down by gunning class, decorative class, etc, and Jason entered the gunning division. That part of the competition is broke down by species. He competed in the Surf Scoter division and took first place. You have to enter a trio, and he did two drakes and one hen. I was so proud and sure wished I was there to see it. On special occasions he will float these birds and today was one of those times. They seem light and fragile, but amazingly enough these hollowed out cedar beauties have withstood the rough conditions of many hunts.

The goal now was to let Jason take the first four drakes. He again would be on photo detail the rest of the way. Dave and I stood ready for back up and cripples. Immediately we had birds in the rig. For every drake we decoy, we have to sift through dozens of juveniles and hens. Dave has nicknamed the juveniles as "roasters", a name that has stuck. One such roaster, or so I thought, was heading straight in.

"Jay, no shot, no shot." I said excitedly while scanning for other possible birds.

"No, it's a Black!" Dave cried out.

"No Jay, a roaster, don't shoot!" I was certain. Juvenile Surf drakes have a bit of yellow in the bill and it is easy to get confused. Black Scoters are really rare in our waters, and to top it off, we had never seen one at this predominate Surf spot.

"Shoot it, shoot it!" Dave continued to yell. At that point he had seen enough, and realizing the Otto's boys were going to let him go, he pulled up and shot the bird. It was a pillow of a shot at about ten yards.

"Dave, what did you do? That is so going to cost you!" I couldn't believe he shot a young bird on opening day. I had already messed up our all drake limits by shooting that Cinnamon and now he had gone and done this? The whole purpose of shooting Scoters on opening day was for their color, they are in perfect plumage in October unlike most other fowl.

"It is a stinking Black, are you guys blind?" He was now astonished we didn't see it. He was laughing out loud and couldn't wait to be vindicated. We quickly threw the buoys and motored over to the dead bird lying face down in the water. In Jay's excitement he ran right over the top of it, too fast for me to scoop him up. The bird popped up at the stern by Jason and he hauled him into the boat.

"A-ha! The great Otto brothers got schooled by the wily old steely eyed guide! I love it!" Sure enough, it was a Black Scoter. It was a beautiful perfect drake at that. I was stunned. How did I miss that? Worse yet, why didn't I shoot it first!

"Wow, nice job Dave. I stand corrected, you are the man. I guess you will have some good luck this year after all," I said in sheer disbelief.

"Thank you, thank you. What do you mean "good luck after all"?"

Jason just shook his head knowing what I was talking about. He then gave me a look. I knew that look. I just smiled hoping he would forgive me for calling him off that Black.

We motored back to the dekes and got reorganized. To shoot a Black Scoter on opening day was an amazing feat for us. To shoot one at that spot was even stranger. That made the whole day, right there.

"Jay, on your right, and no Blacks this time!"

Jason pulled up and sent two drake Surfs crashing into the waves, a fine double. Before we could pull up stakes and pick them up, another flock came locked in and he pulled out another double. I managed to pick off a fleeing bird and just like that we had five drakes in the water. Jason's day was done and it was now time for the camera. For Dave and me it was a different story. It would take another hour and a half to finish out our limits and some rather poor shooting on my part. When hunting birds that fly so low to the water you really know when you miss. Catching up to a target moving at 60 mph with a tailwind is a daunting task at times and watching your spay of pellets run behind the bird over the water can be a little embarrassing. Dave on the other hand wanted to wait out for a drake White Wing Scoter to complete the Scoter Slam, one of each of the three species. This is a special deal to us sea duck hunters, and on the west coast a difficult task to complete. All three of us had done it several times in the past when the Blacks were more plentiful, but it had been a while since I had seen it done and was willing to wait it out. It was not to be and when his patience ran out, he finished on another nice drake Surf.

On the boat ride back I had a time to reflect on the good fortune of the day. I looked down at the big, bulky drake Surfs and picked one up to admire. The bulbous colorful beak is one of the most outrageous characteristics in all of waterfowl. They way they use it to pry off prey shellfish underwater are simply amazing. Other than the white head and back of the neck patches, the rest of the bird is a sheer dark black. When the sunlight hits these birds they tend to shine. On the water, on a nice sunny day, the Surf will glow something unbelievable. I put him down and picked up Dave's Black. He also has that sheer look to him, and his plumage is completely black, from head to toe. He is the only duck in the world with an all black plumage. The neck feathers vermiculate like that of a Snow Goose giving him a rich, full appearance. The chunky bill has a large yellow-orangish color at the base, something I should have, and normally do, see in flight. Scoters are amazing ducks, and we are lucky to have access to them here in Washington.

With day one of hunts under our belt, it was time to travel to the Olympic Peninsula for the second leg of our weekend. I had called Chris at the boat launch and learned they were already en route after a successful day at the "Doctors Property". They had managed three limits of Green Wing Teal and wanted to be in charge of cooking dinner. To this I said amen. I was getting tired and hungry and knew how good it was going to taste. It also meant we were going to be able to save all our meat for an upcoming feast. You can never have enough duck meat!

We arrived first at Captain Dave's compound. Chris and Kasey got there about an hour later. Dave lives deep into the woods in a rustic log house, far from the bright lights and noises of urban development. On the back acreage there are two cabins where his clients and guests stay. These are exceptional cabins. Jason and I always enjoy staying in them. They are decorated with bird mounts of my creation and Ducks Unlimited art, plus he has them loaded with hunting DVD's. All in all it is a perfect place to host an event. Chris immediately began preparing and cooking the Teal while the rest of us got ready for the next day. Dave's two young boys, Spencer and Elliott, came down to inspect the birds and gave us a hand cleaning them. After that we set up for one of our main traditions in the shop, our poker game. During an average season the five of us will get to play three or four games, sometimes being joined by others. I really enjoy playing Texas Holdem', and playing with the same guys all through the year adds an element of strategy you won't get at any pick up game. I find that most Waterfowlers play like they hunt and I will leave it at that.

Freshly barbequed Teal, a good group of friends, and poker... I can't image a better way to spend an evening. The ante tonight was a box of shells, and given the way I had shot that day I wouldn't have minded winning. Dave's wife Tiffany had fixed all the trimmings for the night and was an excellent host. We all really enjoy reliving the days hunt and we had a lot to talk about. Between the five of us we had shot thirty five birds, making for thirty five memorable stories. The games and conversation lasted into the wee hours of the night, until we realized that the next day was fast approaching.

The next morning was a hard get up. That alarm came as soon as my head hit the pillow, I swear. In my groggy state I didn't realize Jason was already up and ready to go.

"Get up, sunshine."

"I am trying, oh man, can I have another ten minutes!" I begged.

"John, one word, Harlequins."

That was all it took. I bounced out of bed and was ready in seconds flat. This morning was all about the elusive blue duck and I couldn't wait. Better yet, we had someone who had never shot a Harlequin going on the hunt. Chris had spent the last couple of seasons trying his luck in several different places but had come up empty. Kasey did manage to score on one of their trips and was no Harly virgin. I was honored to mount his bird during the off season and looked forward to working on Chris' bird. Looking at Kasey's trophy was a reminder to Chris of his lack of success and he wanted that changed. Today would hopefully be the day and his harvest was our main focus.

This morning would be a little more relaxing. Our boat was left back at the cabins so we could use "Big Gray". I thoroughly enjoy hunting out of Dave's boat and like the unusual task of being first mate rather than co-skipper with Jason. Like the day before for Dave, it is a pretty rare occurrence we can afford such luxury of sitting back and watching someone else run the show. Dave's "Big Gray" is a comfortable 19 foot welded aluminum deep "V" style boat that is extremely safe and stable, allowing him to handle all types of weather conditions, which is perfect for running a business on the large and open waters of the Peninsula. Chris and Kasey also brought their boat, an 18 foot sled, so we would have lots of space and comfort. After we both launched, they followed closely behind and we trekked the hour or so run in the dark. Our spot for the morning was a long rocky beach that came to a jutting point that shot right back to the main land. We would park and anchor our boats on the inside of this point to keep them from view and actually hunt on the land. The Harlequins used this beach for their morning congregation before dispersing to other areas to feed. Dave always referred to this behavior as their morning "coffee stop" while on their way to work. Harlequins are first light movers so we had to make haste once we got there.

We all grabbed our decoy bags and met on the beach where we set the long lines from shore. The water is really shallow and the rocky terrain would be murder on the props. When the decoys were all assembled, we looked in astonishment as we realized what a monster spread we were going to run. We Otto's usually deploy about six to eight birds although we have a few more on hand just in case. Dave always ran about eighteen and Chris and Kasey had an even dozen. This was going to be the largest rig of Harlequin I had ever seen, it was quite exciting. If it was late in the year I would have recommended we only pick a few from each rig and run something smaller to emulate their small flocks, but this was early on. The Harlequins were much more apt to run in larger crowds than any other time. When family groups and flocks return from the rivers to the salt, they stay flocked up until winter when they disperse throughout their range. Our spread may just emulate that, and I was feeling good about our chances. All in all we set a rig of 42 Harlequin decoys. If there has ever been a larger rig in Waterfowling history I had never heard of it.

With the decoys set, Dave took Chris to the far end of the spread and sat with him among the driftwood and the rocks. It is always important to take a first timer and give him a little help picking the best bird. A juvenile Harlequin can resemble a mature bird and if you don't know what you are looking for, you could make a costly mistake. This is costly because the limit is one per year, absolutely no room for error. Besides, it was good practice for Dave to ready himself for calling shots on mature Harlequins all season long with his clients. Jason and I took Kasey to the other end. By the time we had sat down we were already five minutes into the day. Pretty good timing considering all the work involved.

In the first half hour, all that we decoyed were a couple of hens and a few juvies. They would land in our fake flock, play and socialize a bit, and move on. While this was going on the entire time there were Scoters and Mallards flying through and above our heads. Those birds were lucky this morning; the last thing you want to do is leave the decoys to chase down or retrieve something other than a Harlequin. The flights can last only an hour or so and you don't want to miss your opportunity. I could see a slight concerned look on Dave's face as the sun was starting to show. Where are the birds? This was not normal. It was also the first hunt there of the year. Harlequin can move out of an area and never return, did this happen here?

As those questions raced through my mind a large flock coming from the open water caught my eye. It was so large I immediately thought it was Scoters. When they got closer, my mind started to change. Their heads were all tilted and cocked slightly up, a characteristic of only one bird. Sure enough, this entire flock that was heading right for us were all Harlequins. Never before or since had I seen such a large flock on the wing. Later, we would guess it to be 60 to 70 strong. For us long time Harlequin watchers the thought still seems unimaginable. But here it was, locked on our massive spread.

"Is that what I think it is?" Kasey leaned over and asked never taking his eyes of the birds.

"It sure is. I don't believe it." Jason muttered. He was amazed by what he was witnessing.

I looked over at Dave and Chris. All I could see was Dave's out stretched hand pointing at birds. When the flock hit the spread they immediately landed, taking off just as fast. That large of a group got spooky and quickly noticed something was not right. I thought for sure Chris was not going to have a shot. They were so closely knitted together you couldn't risk shooting and dropping more than one bird. I also knew that these birds could be the entire population using this beach and they all decided to come at once. There is a chance they could fly away and be gone the whole day.

I turned my attention once again on the flock. The second I did this I heard the shot. It was a single shot and nothing more. I scanned the water to see one dead drake head down and kicking. We all rushed to the edge of the shore to get a closer look. It turned out that a single male decided to zig when he should have zagged separating him from the rest of the group. Dave immediately called the shot and Chris came through. He waded out and picked up his trophy. It was a perfect specimen. When he got back to us I could see he was visibly shaken. Dave's eyes were as big as saucers.

"Did you see that?" Dave yelled in excitement.

We all stood there for a while in utter amazement. I think we would have stayed there all morning discussing that flock but a lone bird sent us scurrying back to the logs to hide. It was a hen but it got us back to hunting. Chris came over to our spot and Kasey joined up with Dave. The Harly was laid out on a log so we could all enjoy. It was an exceptional bird. The white on the tertails was brilliant matching all the white stripes and spots. The black lines that surround the stripes were crisp. A younger bird would not have such a luster.

"Nice job Chris, way to make that shot count. I was worried you weren't going to get an opportunity," mentioned Jason.

"Thanks, you were worried, try being me!"

It seemed Chris's shot sent the flock into disarray. They were now returning in small little groups from all directions. Had he not shot we may have been done. A pair came directly at us and we could tell it was on. When they reached the decoys the hen kept on going while the drake lifted up to land separating himself.

"Take it Jay!" I shouted. He was already up. His first shot was behind the bird. The second went wildly astray. The third was once again behind the now fleeing drake. I was ready for back up and lit one off. My shot sent him tumbling head over heals into the water. It was sweet, I rarely get a chance to back him up like that, and I thoroughly enjoyed it.

"Nice shot! You are going to remind me of this all day now aren't you?"

"Isn't that what brothers are for?" We both laughed as I went out and got my bird. Another prime bull and it felt good. I put it up with Chris's bird on the log and preened it nicely for the impending pictures.

On the other end of the spread a trio came in. I could see Kasey pull up and drop his bird right on the beach, it must have been only ten yards away. The shot sent the other drake of the trio right back to us. When he got to the edge Jason took a shot and missed, putting his gun down.

"What happened?"

"Just didn't feel right. I am going to move down the way to the edge and hunt by myself if you guys don't mind." I could see his miss frustrated him a bit, and going solo was probably his best medicine. Hunting Harly's can get stressful at times and it doesn't help that there are now three prime drakes on the log to view. Kasey had now joined us so I walked down to keep an alone Dave company.

"Nice guiding Captain. You look like you are in late season form there. Getting Chris that shot must have been something."

"Let me tell you Johnny boy, I still can't believe that drake peeled off. The Captain got lucky and spotted that one."

Moments later I heard a shot and looked down the way to see Jason had a bird down. I could then hear a "wahoo" of excitement as he joined the others at the log. We now had four birds down and only one to go.

"You know John," Dave told me with a very spiritual look on his face. "I don't think I am going to pull the trigger on a blue duck today. I think I will take a pass for good karma for the season. We got four nice birds to enjoy; five would be just one more."

"Are you sure?" I was a little disappointed but totally understood. The thought of a five person limit sure sounded nice, but you just can't push certain things and this seemed like one of them.

"Positive. Let's pick up this rig and hit the White Wings while they are still flying." Just as he said that a lone drake dumped into the decoys. It was like on cue, almost as if Mother Nature was testing his wish for good karma. The bird just began to play around and swim contently with the corkers.

"Are you really sure? There he is . . ."
"Positive."

And with that we picked up. Dave would go on to finish the season and not take his drake all year. The karma paid off, he finished another year running his clients at 100% harvest success rate, keeping his streak alive since he started his business. Given all the factors that go hand in hand in waterfowl hunting, I have always thought that streak to be amazing. Maybe his decision that day had a difference. Or maybe it is just hard work and skill.

The White Wings were about a mile away and we were set up and ready to go in no time. I finished the day with two nice bull drakes and a couple of Mallards that ventured too close to the open water spread. The rest of the crew finished out with a nice string of drakes as well, although none of us got a limit. This day belonged to the Harlequin, the rest was just cream. I took all the Harlequins and later that week mounted them all for the guys. I took Dave's skin from the prior year so I could do five mounts to remember the days hunt. Chris was especially excited to get his first Harly mount, and he retired one of the cedar decoys he had made and hunted that day to sit along side his bird on his mantle.

That night I arrived home at about 10:00 and to say that I was tired was an understatement. I barely had enough energy to say "hi" to Toni before I crashed. The kids were all in bed at this point and their hugs had to wait until the morning. As I mentioned earlier, we judge this weekend by how tired we are when we are done. Well, given the circumstance of my exhaustion, we were extremely successful. I knew I would get to work a little late the next day and the thought of sitting at my desk felt good. I know that when I look forward to work so I can relax a bit that I have achieved ultimate success. The season was now underway, and this would quickly become a memory, a very good memory at that.

Chapter 6

Pheasants, Dogs and My Hero

The amount of time, and the trips I have dedicated to pheasant hunting in the last decade, seems to have followed the life cycle of my lab, Comet. Chasing roosters is a commitment to us West side guys, due to the fact the best areas are four to six hours away, and you have to go over a mountain pass to get to the east side. When she was a puppy, we only went a couple of times. When she started to hit her prime at three years old, and on to about six or seven, I tried to go as often as we could, sometimes spending several weekends in a row going east. As she began to decline, so unfortunately did the trips. I found myself this year with no dog at all, a first for me since I was a teenager. I wasn't even sure if I could muster the excitement level needed for travel, and I knew it would break my heart to leave Comet behind. There was no way I could bring her, but that selfish thought did cross my mind a few times.

This year the pheasant opener happens to fall on the weekend after the duck opener. This is a good thing for those who like to do both. Some years they fall on the same weekend and I know several people who have to really put some thought into what they want to do. Early in my hunting career it was a no brainer, pheasants. Waterfowl easily wins out nowadays, but only because of circumstance.

Pheasant hunting was what I was raised up with, its how I cut my teeth. At eight years old my Dad would let me tag along with my BB gun, even letting me think I got a bird or two. I absolutely loved it. At a young age I shot my first rooster in Royal City, while hunting with Tar, our legendary Lab. Tar is more than a legend in our family. I would say she has been elevated to icon status. Every dog after has been compared to her, fairly or unfairly, and as time goes by I can't see any pups getting a legitimate shot. The boxes of Field Trial ribbons and pictures of dead game posed in front of her are forever etched in my mind.

When she passed, it destroyed my Dad. That was a day I will never forget. It also temporarily put out his fire for hunting. A few years later Jason would get his Lab Jordy, another legend. Jordy enabled me and Jason to start hunting again, and we concentrated on waterfowl. A couple of years later, I would get Comet. This inspired Dad, and after a couple of trips east to hit the covers with our two dogs he was once again hooked. When I bred Comet with a stud dog he was really fond of, Dad got one of the puppies and named her Teal. I love Teal, she is my Band-Tail buddy.

As Teal developed into one of the finest pheasant dogs that ever lived, you couldn't keep us three out of those cut corn fields and wheat stubble. If only dogs could live as long as us. Jordy passed a couple of years ago, breaking up the team. This was certainly a blow, and it seems our trips have cycled down since. My Dad has often said that Jordy single handedly inspired us all to come back to the sport we all love. She was a living testament to the power of a dog.

Jason knew I was reluctant to go with out Comet and came over to the house to have a chat. He was somewhat in the same boat having a rookie dog but was feeling quite inspired. I was in full duck mode and could think of a million of opportunities just waiting to be hit. He began to talk of all the trips we had in our past, bringing up memories I hadn't thought of in a while. If anyone knew how to get to me it was Jason, and it wasn't very hard for him to push his agenda. All that he needed to do was discuss the opportunity to hang out with Dad. I love our hunts with him. Packing up the rig, the drive over, the overnight stay in the hotel room we always cram ourselves into, those are the real parts of a pheasant trip I cherish. Of course I would go, even if it meant leaving Comet behind. A bitter truth about being a wing shooter and involving dogs is the cycle of their life, and moving on is a part of that process.

Friday night we packed up and headed out. We decided on some ground in Dusty Washington, about an hour south of Colfax which was on the far eastern side of the state. There are two farms that we have hunted for years, the Largent's and Darlene's. Both are unique and hold thousands of untouched acres, all open for our enjoyment. The Largent's farm is largely made up of wheat fields. These fields are spotted all around the many hills in the area. At some points the hills are too steep to farm, creating what we call "eyebrows" of cover. Thick and hard to hunt, they hold more game than just pheasants and other game birds. More often than not we have kicked out some world class White-Tail deer. Darlene's, on the other hand, is a worn down farmstead made up mostly of CRP. We also have permission to hunt her neighboring farm, a place we call Fritz's. This was more of the same, CRP for as long as the eye could see. Both areas have their own set of challenges and can hold a lot of birds.

We got there on Friday in time to enjoy a little daylight for scouting. It was good to see a couple of roosters sitting in the corners of the fields. Now I was really starting to get in the mood. I figured I would share my time with Dad and Teal, and wander back to Jason and Ruddy, kind of poach both of their dogs during the day. The hotter of the two dogs just might see my mug more, and hey, anyone hunting without a dog for pheasants has to turn into an opportunist, right?

The morning started out a bit slow, unusual for an opening day. We started out by hunting the eyebrows, which was really to my benefit. I would hike to the end and block while they would push through the cover. This worked well for two reasons. Number one, the birds that would run and flush at the end of the cover, out of range of the pushers, were met with a gun they weren't suspecting. The second was if the opposite happened, they notice the blocker. Sometimes to a pheasant the thought of some one ahead helps them hold, they get the feeling they are surrounded. This is mostly a late season strategy, but without a dog I made myself as useful as possible. The lack of pressure had the birds holding tight and Jason and Dad quickly had a rooster each in the pouch.

My first bird would come around noon, ironically enough while on a hike to block. I was walking the edge when a couple of hens flushed. Knowing the roosters hold a little tighter, I did a quick run into the bush, kicking up two males that were hoping I would keep walking. I dropped one on my first shot, and quickly missed the second with my remaining two shots. I was shooting my Remington 1100 20 gauge, the very gun my Dad bought for me when I was ten. The same gun I used to shoot my first rooster.

After we grew weary of climbing the steep hillsides that held the eyebrows, we gave our attention to the bits of cover lying in between the wheat stubble. The nice level walking felt good. Good that is until Ruddy caught scent. The cover was really thin, and there was nothing to block a rooster from running, and run he did. Both Jason and I took off on the chase, only small pauses for Ruddy to hunt around and catch scent again. I could see the patch end soon and knew something was going to give. I decided to slow down and let Jason finish it out. As soon as they got to the edge, the rooster exploded straight up. He was quickly met by the steel shot of a Beretta 303 20 gauge, and tumbled down to earth. Ruddy was right on it for a quick retrieve. Once in hand we all took a knee to show Ruddy our gratitude . . . and to rest a bit!

My second and third bird came on a nice double. I rarely get to record a double on pheasants and was really excited I was able to have the opportunity. They flushed while walking a patch of CRP that was cresting over a small rolling hillside while hunting with Teal and Dad. It was a group of about ten birds that Teal had methodically worked for over a hundred yards. I picked the first bird that broke the farthest to my left, dropped him, and then refocused on the next rooster I could find. Lucky for me it was a nice straight away lifting directly in front of me. I took two shots, got two birds, which is also a rare occurrence when I am involved. In all my commotion I didn't realize Dad had taken his second bird out of the same flock. Jason heard the shooting and appeared over the crest. We had temporarily separated and he too had picked up his limit bird. It wasn't too often Dad found himself the last to need a bird and we knew he would be hunting hard until he got it.

At this point Jason and I just hiked behind him with Ruddy at heel, letting Teal do all the work. I watched my Dad, his face full of intensity. He takes nothing light, and upland hunting is something he approaches with a bulldog attitude. I enjoy his tenacity, his drive, and his challenging of nature. Teal had it too; both of them were working with a sync born from years of experience. We scoured the fields, kicking up only a couple of hens. I hiked on with a strange confidence, Dad never left without his bird.

We came up to a small draw that wound uphill through a stubble field. We had a few more opportunities, but time was running out fast. Darkness would be coming soon. The cover started out rather wide, and got skinnier as we neared the end. Dad motioned for me to go block. I knew what he was thinking; stop that runner from peeling out before we could get to the end. I hiked up the hill as far away from the cover as I could, as to not scare anything prematurely. I also had to hike fast, we were running out of real estate and if I didn't get there in time it would all be pointless.

I arrived out of breath. Nothing makes you feel more out of shape than a good upland hunt, especially when so many hills were involved. A bend in the draw did not allow me to see them marching until they were about two hundred yards away. The closer they came, the more I realized their pace was a bit hurried. Teal was on scent. She was zigzagging left to right, stopping and starting again. This was no hen, and for sure no first year bird. I wondered if it would run wild. I quickly made the decision to pace back and forth a bit, hoping to keep the bird in the cover. I didn't want to make too much noise and flush it wild, just enough to let him know running out wasn't safe.

When they got to about fifty yards out, Teal froze. It wasn't a point, but I can only imagine that the big old rooster had had enough and was at the end of his rope. There they stood, face to face.

"Teal get the bird!" Dad said in a loud whisper.

Teal pounced on the bush. A cascade of cackles erupted as the old bird leapt skyward. Tail feathers were everywhere, chaos all around. My eyes were on Dad. He was ready. The gun was up, his head was down, and I watched him begin to follow the flying mess of feathers. Bang! He kept his follow through. The bird crashed down onto the stubbled hillside, stone dead. I will never forget the look on his face, a look of pure satisfaction. He walked out of the cover and met Teal in the stubble. One hand took the bird as she heeled and the other was quickly in her muzzle giving her praise on a job well done.

I look back to his face. For the first time I begin to notice some of the effects of age. His hair was starting to gray. I am lucky, I was born when he was young and plan on spending many more days like this in the future. But at that moment I saw my Dad as more than just that, I saw him as my hero. The tenacity he showed in getting that last bird is something he instilled in his boys. Not just in hunting, but in the game of life. Everything I have ever accomplished I owe to the example of this man. I was lucky enough to really experience a moment of watching it all come together on this hunt. The hard work, the planning, the split second reactions, and the spoils of victory, this hunt was a metaphor for how he has lived his life. I was very proud to be his son. He didn't know it, but the hug I walked up to give him was not for a nice shot on that pheasant, but for the years of life lessons he has taught me, and how much I appreciate him.

The walk down the hill back to the farm was exhilarating. Dad has always told us happiness was the weight you feel on your back when the strap is full of birds. I could feel the weight of my three pheasants and at that moment nothing was finer. The dogs were happy and tired, but still managed to dance all the way back to camp. I was looking forward to a nice cold beer in the hotel room and watching a little baseball. It is mid October and the playoffs are in full swing, it just doesn't get better than this.

The next day was a lot slower, as is mostly the case during opening weekends in the uplands. Dad scored a couple of nice birds, and Ruddy worked up Jay a real beauty. Those three on the opener were all I would score. I was a bit sad driving home as I knew it would be a while before I would return. My dog was done, and I wasn't sure when the next one was coming. The only thing I did know for sure was that there was going to be another dog in my future, and there will be more pheasant hunts. These trips were way too important to let slip away. We need another crew of three dogs to get us all inspired again. All I want is to be able to tap into the magical power of a well trained dog, and spend more time with my hero.

Chapter 7

Banded Barrows and Rough Seas

The Barrows Goldeneyes come in to Puget Sound like clockwork every year. For all the years we have tracked them with our hunting logs, the date they arrive may vary by one or two days at the most. With this for margin of error, I would say that it is as solid as it gets. The magic date for us is October 22nd. We have sort of a ritual to be on a certain beach in Skagit Bay on this day and have never been disappointed. The beach is private and belongs to a fellow who lives above the cliff that is directly behind the beach, seated deep into the woods. The only favor he asks of us is to swing by on this date every year and show him the Barrows we are lucky enough to harvest. Of course we comply and have so for quite some time. We have named the spot in honor of the large chunky Goldeneye, and call it Barrows Beach.

We will hunt this spot a few times a year, but mostly as a last resort. The little cove it sits in is protected from all winds except a true northern. This is a nice option if we have winds and can't get out, a perfect plan "b". It has saved many a hunt. If there is a good eastern or western, many different birds come right to the dekes that wouldn't normally come so close to shore just to get out of whatever storm we are avoiding as well. Other than Barrows we have taken Surf Scoters, White-Wing Scoters, Black Scoter, Harlequin, both Scaup, Common Goldeneye, Wigeon, Mallard, Gadwall, and even a few

Green-Wing Teal. Not too many scoter hunters can say they shot these sea ducks off the beach, and we have taken folks there just for that reason.

In 2001, Jason had to miss the last month of the season to finish out his college degree back east in New Jersey, at Rutgers University. It was a strange month for me being without my brother and partner. All the things that become routine became quite confusing. We have developed a definite structure and each of us has our own roles and jobs. I took a few guests out and would notice dumb little things not getting done, like putting the plug in the boat. Yes, on one hunt I forgot to put the plug in the boat. This has always been Jason's job and with him not there, I had to think for both of us, which at times is not a good thing for me. The boat took on quite a bit of water before I noticed, and it took a lot of sweat and bilging to get it out. In recent years we have tried to mix up our little "duties" so when we hunt without each other we don't have this problem. I have found that it is best to simply not go without him.

Anyway, I was on a hunt on the last day of that season in 2001 with a friend by the name of Dave Kilmer. We had intended to launch at his private beach in Madrona at the southern tip of Camano Island and do a little Surf Scoter hunting. We had a pounding east wind punching right at us and it was impossible to even back the boat down let alone launch. I quickly suggested we run over to our Barrows Beach for a last ditch effort at a hunt.

Once we got there the east was still kicking. I looked through the binoculars to see that our beach was as calm as could be. All we had to do was get there; the launch is only about a half mile from our destination. We launched and stuck close to shore until we rounded the point that protected our spot and found smooth sailing from there. That day the birds were not flying too well, the storm had most birds out in the open water waiting it out. We had a few Barrows, a couple of White-Wings and a Surf and decided that after next bird we shot we would pick up and call it a day. The waves seemed to be getting a little more violent and I didn't want to fight it, especially on the last day of the season. As soon as I mention this a flock of Barrows set right in. All were hens and juveniles except one lone drake. It was my turn, so I pulled up and shot at the bird, sailing him directly into the waves. All I could think was, "nice shot dummy".

We picked our gear, fought the surf for the bird, and headed back. After a long struggle to get the boat on the trailer, both Kilmer and I took a breather in the parking lot, happy to be off the water. He went over and picked up the Barrows to get a closer look at the plumage. What we didn't notice while fighting the waves was this bird was banded. Our first ever banded Barrows Goldeneye. I immediately called my brother on the cell phone to tell him of my fortune. As you can imagine, he was just so excited for me. Here he was stuck in New Jersey and I am out shooting banded Goldeneyes. I felt a little guilty about this, of course, and when he got home I gave him the band. He collects them on his call lanyard and a Barrows would be a nice addition. I usually leave them on the bird and then mount it. I had plenty of Barrows mounted in my trophy room so this was perfect. I felt better, and he thought I was pretty cool. I mean what are big brothers for, right?

Fast forward to this season, October 22nd to be exact, and we were making a plan. We did as we always do and set out for Barrows Beach. As usual, we still had not seen a Barrows yet this season but knew they would be there. It was a calm October morning without a cloud in the sky and the weather for the day was to be warm with no wind. I have a certain internet site bookmarked that gave the marine forecasts and it is almost always spot on. Almost always.

We had paddled over in our Aqua-Pods instead of taking our boat. The travel distance was so short from the boat launch it seemed like a good idea at the time. We brought a dozen cedar and cork Barrows each, perfect for a little cove hunt.

My rig consisted mostly of decoys I had carved with a few mixed in from Jason. I did however have a nice little four pack of corkers from carver Gary March who hunts out of Spokane. Gary is a legendary die hard Goldeneye hunter on the rivers in Eastern Washington, and I really wanted some decoys from him in my collection. A couple of years earlier he donated a whole six pack complete with weights and a nice bag to our Washington Brant Foundation for our auction and I had to have them. I ended up trading two of them to Drewry leaving me with just the four. Those are among my favorites. Jason's rig was entirely made up his own carvings except for one. Carver Don Spidell, who lives in our home town, had done a trade carve with him a year earlier. Don is also a fervent Goldeneye hunter, and carves a mean Barrows. Also in Jason's rig was a Common that earned him first place ribbon in state event down in Vancouver a year earlier. I really liked this decoy, although it made me nervous to shoot over. It was cedar and hollowed out and you don't want to shoot that! He would always say the same thing, "I know a guy who can fix it." I love that line.

A SEASON OF WING-SHOOTING

We couldn't have had a smoother start, the tide was perfect, the weather was mild, and the decoys went out nice and smooth. We drug down a large log to sit on and hid our Pods in the undergrowth along the edge of the cliff. Sure enough, right with the early light, the first Barrows of the season decoyed with his mate. The sound of whistling from his wings was melodic, the year since I had last heard it had been to too long. I cleanly took him letting the Suzie scamper to the middle of the sound. The great thing about shooting Barrows so early in the season is the plumage. Goldeneyes feather up early and the drakes are in perfect shape as soon as they arrive.

The action got slow after that. We managed to decoy a few more hens and juveniles in the first hour, but no more drakes. That is when the wind began to pick up. No big deal we thought, we were only a few hundred yards from our truck, let's stick it out. Then another hour went by, still no birds and more wind. The strangest part about it was the wind was coming directly out of the north. There was no mention of this on the marine forecast, and I certainly would never have guessed to have such a wind in October. The lack of birds was rather normal and we expected that. It can take a few weeks for all of them to trickle up to the numbers we have come to enjoy.

The white caps that were starting to form got us a bit nervous so we finally decided to call it a day. I was pretty happy we at least got one Barrows, our annual date didn't let us down, and we saw others. The tide had dropped in our favor and we were able to wade out and grab the long lines by hand, so we started to pick up. I was about waist deep fighting waves when a lone Barrows drake came barreling, lucky for Jason he was still standing on the beach. I was off to the left of him and the bird was coming in from my direction. This was perfect, by the time he noticed me he veered right, but it was too late. Jason had grabbed his gun and only needed to wait until it cleared. His first shot took the top off a wave that was about a three footer; the second rang true and sent him into the chop head down. That was the good thing, thank god he killed it dead. The bad thing was he now was going to have to fight with his Pod to retrieve his bird. We had left Ruddy at home for this hunt so the Pod ride was more comfortable. This was probably a good thing anyhow as it would not have been good for her to be swimming in those waves.

He quickly grabbed his Pod, cleaned off all the leaves and branches that were concealing it, and drug the small boat down to the beach. I saw him do a quick look to make sure he had his life vest on, which he did, and he started in. The bird was only about forty yards out by this time, but it looked like it was a mile. I ran and got my Pod ready in case he needed any help. Getting through the surf was the hardest part; he had to time the waves. I would say he did it about half right, and the water that was now soaking him attested to that. He looked back and flashed me a smile.

"Oh man, that is cold!"

"Be careful!" I yelled at him. I was only ten yards away but the wind had kicked up so fierce he could barely hear me. I started to get a little stressed.

Up and down he went until he reached the bird. I saw him make a quick grab at its head and miss. Stopping for just that split second had him immediately out of range of grabbing it again and he had to fight to reposition himself for another swipe. This time I saw a handful of wing and feathers, he wasn't messing around. He took one quick turn of the oar and he was heading back in the right direction. The current took him about a hundred feet down the beach. At first he tried to fight the waves to angle back to where I was waiting. This just wasn't working so he took a straight shot back to shore. Once there he realized there were a bunch of fallen logs and drift wood dancing in the surf.

"Ahhh, dangit!" I could barely hear him shout at the top of his lungs.

I watched as his Pod hit the first log and shot the boat to the right side. He was only in knee to ankle deep water depending on the timing of the waves crashing in so he jumped out. This sent the Pod upside down, his gear went scattering. I ran over as fast as I could on shore to help him.

"Are you o.k.?" I yelled as I came up on him.

"Not a scratch, don't loose my Barrows!"

I had to chuckle even though there was a bit of chaos going on. We Otto boys are a little particular about our game, sometimes to our detriment. Bird is always first, worry about the rest later.

"I see it floating, I'll get it!" I took a wave right in the face as I bent down to grab him. Jason in the mean time had managed to get his Pod safely on the beach. We then gathered up what little gear he had scattered in the surf. The only damage to the Pod was a broken oar holder.

"Now that was a bit dumb, I think next time I will let him fly on out of here." Jason said with a very relieved look on his face. I quickly nodded with agreement.

I gave the bird a good shake while holding his bill to get all the water off. If you do this you can get the bird to look nice and fluffy and clean. Leaving all the water to penetrate the down and you will have a drowned rat in your hands. I knew Jason was going to want to sit for a spell and admire his first Barrows of the year, might as well have it look good.

I laid the bird down on a log and walked back to get mine from earlier. It was smoking time. I pulled out a couple of victory cigars. We knew we would be on the beach for a while, there was no way we were going to fight those waves back to the launch. Also, there was a large log half in the water blocking any type of walking back a few hundred yards down beach. I figured we would either have to wait for the wind to calm, or the tide to drop another few feet so we could walk around the log.

Jason flung his wet cap off into the sand, sat down, and gave his cigar a big long draw. He reached over and grabbed his trophy for the day to give it the once over.

"Waaahooo!!" He jumped up and started whooping. I jumped up with him to see what all the excitement was about. It was banded. How did I miss that?

I couldn't help but make the comparisons to the bird I had shot. Both were on an extremely windy day, both at the exact same spot. Both birds were not noticed with a band until later, which never happens. On the beach we compared the two numbers to see that they were only *22 numbers apart*, banded on the same day at Riske Creek up in far northern Canada. We would later become friends with the biologist from the CFW while helping him work on a Brant project. He had banded both birds, his name is Sean Boyd. He invited us up one year to help in Riske, but we couldn't get away from work. Instead we sent him a carved cork decoy Jason made and a few skins. They wanted to use the skins to decoy the birds into the traps, this did not work. The water simply tore them to shreds. What did work was Jason's decoy, and it worked well. It felt good to give back a little after taking two birds from his study.

I leaned over to him while sitting on that beach and asked him, "So, now that you have shot a banded Barrows do you suppose I could have my band back?"

"Nope."

Chapter 8

A Brothers Challenge

It was late Friday night and I hadn't made a plan with Jason for the next morning. All I knew was the fact that we would be somewhere and didn't think much else of it. This isn't unusual for us. We have been known to make up our minds at the last second, sometimes even waiting until we are on the road. Weather conditions can dictate, or the time of year, or simply what we feel like holding in our hands on that particular day. When we depart in the mornings we usually are prepared for anything. I was just about asleep on the couch when the phone rang.

"Hello?" I could see that is was Captain Dave by the caller I.D. It was late, and I was bit surprised to hear from him.

"Hey John, you and Jason want some company tomorrow?" he replied sounding very upbeat.

"You bet, don't you have clients?"

"Nope," he answered. "I got a clean day!"

He went on to tell me how he had mentally screwed up his own schedule, thinking they were coming in on Friday to hunt Saturday. They were actually planned for a day behind and this "bonus" time had him quite excited. It was getting rare to have a day to himself where he wasn't too tired to get out there. His business was booming so well he has hunts that butt up right next to each other in an effort to squeeze them all in, barely giving him even time to sleep.

"I want to take Bill as well, he needs a good shoot." Bill was Dave's brother that had recently moved north to Bainbridge Island from Southern California. He had come up to visit about a year earlier and just like that decided to uproot his family and head north. The city life in Southern Cal was starting to take a toll on him. He felt raising his two boys in the rural of Washington was a much better upbringing. I respect a decision like that. He had a thriving business that he sold and basically had to start over. Bill is a good man and I really like his company in the blind.

"Sounds great, what should we target?" I asked. Heck, neither Jason nor I had a plan, let's make Dave create one.

"You know what, let's go anywhere where there is a lot of variety. Variety is the key. I want to see as many different birds as possible."

I had the perfect place in mind.

"Wigeon Cove, what do you think?" This would mean they had to come over the ferry to meet up. Not a big deal and I knew when I mentioned this he would be excited. Wigeon Cove is nestled in to one of the first bays coming off of the Strait of Juan de Fuca separating the U.S. mainland from Vancouver Island. All sorts of different species congregate here early in the season before spilling south into the Puget Sound. This should give him the variety he was looking for.

"Done, perfect! Meet us at the ferry docks and we will caravan over. First boat arrives at six and this should give us just enough time for first light." The plan was made.

The next morning I picked up Jason at his house and filled him in on all the details. We decided to take every decoy we owned; we wanted to be ready for anything. Over a hundred cork and cedar decoys is quite a haul, and we knew we would have to work fast to drop them all and still make first light with the handicap of meeting them at the dock. That is when we started talking. Today would be a good day to attempt something we had talked about for years but had never got around to completing all the way. We were going to go for the goal of shooting a seven different drake limit. To get this done you needed two things. First, you have to have the right conditions. The spot we were going to hunt was prime and waiting for such an attempt. Second, you needed patience, lots of patience. We felt we were up to the task and welcomed such a lofty goal. I knew of a few folks who had accomplished this and in all cases it just sort of happened. You look down at what you have and realize if you get a little selective to finish out it could be done. But to start the day not wavering and sticking to the goal was going to be hard. We had done it plenty of times in the 80's when bird numbers were down due to all the droughts, and the limit was a mere four birds. But this was seven, much different.

After meeting up with the boys and getting to the launch we told them of our goal. I could see the little wheels churning in Dave's mind.

"Oh yeah, we are in too. I love it. In fact, I bet we can come closer to doing this than you guys can!" Dave said seeing if he could spark a little competition.

Oh boy, a challenge. I love a challenge and Dave knows it.

I quickly blurted, "You're on. We will show you guys what brothers rule the waters out here." I looked over at Jason, who gave me a shrug and nod of confidence. "This will be easy. My little four year old daughter Kaden has more patience than both Drewry brothers combined."

"If you guys are so sure of yourselves, let's make it interesting. Loser buys lunch at Toby's." Bill added. This was a funny bet they were proposing. Both those guys are the type of person that no matter what the situation is you have to wrestle the tab away to pay. We are the same way. Generosity is definitely their strong suit and I have had many humorous arguments with them on this subject. It is kind of a running joke who can grab the bill first. I have even gone as far as strategizing with the waitress to sneak it to me when no one was looking.

"Done." Jason quipped rather quickly. And with that, we both launched and headed out.

Dave and Bill were going to hunt a point that was about a quarter mile south of the beach and just beyond Wigeon Cove, where we were. We quickly dropped the rig as best we could and scurried back to the blind. I think a line or two crossed under water, starting a nice little cluster, but there was no time to figure it out. The birds were already circling. I could still see a small light running inside Captain Dave's boat as I glassed to see how they were getting along. They are both what we would call "fiddlers", nothing is just quite right and must be messed with until their perceived level of perfection is achieved. I chuckled as I saw the boat bouncing all around. I looked down at my cell phone and it was five minutes after shooting started, not bad.

"Don't shoot! Too tight!" Jason said in a loud whisper. A flock of Teal zipped through the decoys and I barely had time to notice. One shot into that and the goal was long gone right off the bat.

A SEASON OF WING-SHOOTING

Almost immediately the Goldeneyes came. Both Barrows and Commons, which is a little bit unusual, the Commons are mostly a later bird to arrive in this area. I knew this was a good sign. Ten minutes in and we had already seen three species.

"Jay, look right!" I pointed at an incoming pair of Barrows. They twisted and set right in front of him but gave no shot. The hen was acting as a shield as they dumped into the rig. Just before they lit the water they took off straight up giving me a clear shot at the drake. I took one poke and sent him feet up into the water.

My shot seemed like a starting bell to our friends down the way. Seconds later they unleashed a war. I clearly counted six shots. As Ruddy was splashing away retrieving my Goldeneye, I glassed their direction again, in time to see Bay making retrieves, lots of them. What kind of flock did they have come in?

The Goldeneyes started coming in thicker numbers. Trios, duos, solo birds, flocks, all wanted in our space. Patiently Jason carved out both a Common and a Barrows while I too picked up a Common. That was two birds apiece, two different drakes. I started to get worried we were going to miss out on all this Goldeneye shooting, what if nothing else came? Should we give in and have one heck of a shoot?

"Don't even think about it . . ." Jason called over to me as yet another trio of Barrows came setting. He must have read my mind. He carries all the patience in this family, I just wanted to shoot.

A few minutes later I saw them. Two drake Greater Scaup were coming and coming on strong. The second they hit my side of the rig they began to skirt the outer edge. I gave them a quick poke and missed. Jason took a swinging two canoe lead shot at the front bird as they rounded his end and sent him skidding across the water. He was dead on arrival. Ruddy made quick work of the retrieve and he now had three birds, three species.

Once again what sounded like World War three erupted from the Drewry's. This time I counted five rapid shots. That was followed up with a few cripple shots. Bay was again in the water. A few minutes after that, another flurry of shots rang out. I was starting to wonder just how patient these boys were. We were barely a half hour into the hunt. They were either really lucky or shooting rather poorly.

"Puddle ducks, to the right . . ." Jason was watching them like a hawk. As they got closer it was easy to tell, Wigeon, the very species this place got its namesake. A couple of snorts on the call had the entire flock right over us, chaos everywhere. I looked up and picked the nicest drake I could find. My first shot was a miss, I tipped him on the second, and sailed him on the third. My bird landed about 250 yards out with his head up, I knew this was trouble. I looked over at Jason who had not fired a shot.

75

"What happened?" I asked rather hurriedly keeping an eye on my cripple.

"I had no good shot; everything was just to close together. When you took your shot they tightened up even further." I could tell he was frustrated.

I then quickly ran to the boat, which was hidden down the beach, never taking my eye off the Wigeon. I pulled the boat out, started the motor, and ran out there to see him swimming to the open water as fast as he could go. Just when I was close enough to finish him off he dove. I could tell he wasn't going anywhere and relaxed a bit. He was in pretty rough shape and it was obvious. I just turned the motor off and drifted waiting for him to surface. About a half minute later he came up, actually closer to me than before his dive. I quickly gave a dispatch shot and picked him up.

I looked back to the shore to see I had gone quite a ways, I could barely see Jason on the beach. What I could see was a flock circling him. All of a sudden a bird dropped, then another and a second later the shots rang out. I was pretty far out there. I full throttled in dieing to see what he had harvested. Was he done? Did he mean to shoot two?

As soon as I thought I was in voice range I called out, "What did you get?" He still couldn't hear me, but I could see a happy look on his face. I parked the boat and hurried down the beach.

I got there just in time to see Ruddy bringing in the second bird. I could see the head of a bull drake Gadwall draped out of her mouth. What a great sight. The Gadwall is my favorite puddle duck. They look so plain from a small distance away but when you get close you notice all the intricate plumage and feather detail. That and the fact we don't see a lot of Gadwall in the season, especially primed up drakes, made it even more exciting.

"Nice bird Jay!"

"You should see my Wigeon." I looked down on the log where he was storing his birds to see a perfect bull.

"I shot the Wigeon first, and then noticed two drake Gadwalls on the outer edge of the flock trying to escape, I got lucky." He explained.

That was huge. To pull off a goal like this you need a little luck and he just got some. Did I forget to mention that the whole time of our adventure the guns to the south were relentless? Before I sat down in my blind I tried again to glass them. Bay was in the water, which is all I could tell. They were obviously having a good time. Jason now had five ducks, and five different species. He was well on his way. I was still sitting on three.

After the Wigeon flocks there was a bit of a lull. A few more Goldeneye committed but today got free passes. My pocket began to vibrate, my cell phone was going off.

"Hey Dave! You guys got any shells left or what?" I answered.

"You forgot to turn on your two-way, I've been trying to call you. How many more birds do you guys need?" Dave said, half laughing.

"We are getting there, a few more. What the heck have you been shooting at? Are you done?"

"We need one more, let's just say we are having a great shoot." With that answer I could tell he wasn't going to give any details, so I wasn't either. I also knew we better get going or we would have them on our beach teasing us as we shot our last few.

"Cool, well . . . . hey . . ." I had looked to my left to see two drake Hooded Mergansers trying to back door our spread. I threw the cell into the sand and pulled up my gun. Just as I shot, the two birds crossed paths and down they went. I jumped up to see I had scotch doubled, both were floating head down, dead. I was really disappointed. First, my goal was done. Second, if I had just got the one Jason would have surely picked up the other helping him out.

"Well, it was a nice shot!" Jason said obviously noticing my disappointment.

I shrugged my shoulders. I have to say though the feeling quickly disappeared as I held the two birds. I love Hooded Mergansers. We call them "Wood Ducks of the Salt". These two were in perfect plumage and it is not everyday one can say he got to double on Hoodeds. I could hear Dave talking and I discovered I never did hang up my phone. I picked it up to find him eagerly waiting.

"Well, did you get it!"

"Oh yeah, I got them, both of them. One shot!"

"Ooops . . . that can't be good. Get a hen?" Dave holds the same opinion on shooting hens as we do.

"Nope, drakes."

"Then great!" He replied.

There was a little relief. I now had five birds and could take whatever drake I wanted to now, no reason to be picky. The next bird to pile in was a nice Greater Scaup. Jason had to let it go and I was more than happy to add that to the log. I finished up on a nice Barrows. Now it was time to wait and watch Jason. The birds kept coming, just not the right birds.

"Jay, I guarantee we have got more species than those guys, we got the bet in the bag. Shoot away if you want, don't feel like you have too." I was trying to give him a way out if it wasn't what he wanted to do.

"That is where you are wrong, I HAVE too. This is one of those days you think of in the off season. I will be ticked if I don't do this." I totally understood. I have spent many hot summer days reflecting on situations like this, questioning myself on this strategy or on that move. I figure I will probably be thinking about my Hoodeds for quite some time.

Another flock of Wigeons began dancing around just outside the spread. I could see Jason peering and scouring each bird when his eyes lit up. My eyes darted over to see a nice plump greenhead. Jason hadn't shot a Mallard yet, which is probably the duck we decoy most during the season. He started throwing out notes on his call and had him hooked. All alone he set in right on the corner of the spread. One shot sent him downward. The momentum of his flight sent him into the sand, only feet away from Jason. It was a really decent bull that had nice full curls.

A few moments later I heard a shot from the Drewry's. I got on the two-way that I had remembered to turn on and was told they were done. They were knee deep in brother conversation and told us to take our time and they would meet us at the launch when we were done. It was good to hear they were getting some quality time together.

For about an hour we waited. The flights had slowed down and we did have a few close calls. A small flock of Surf Scoters almost came in but spooked at the last second. A lone Black Scoter surprised us from behind and was gone before we knew it. Another Hooded dropped in unnoticed, dove amongst the decoys, and was never seen again. Jason was not wavering. We were in it for the long haul.

Just before 11:00 I spotted a lone duck coming straight in and low from way out in the bay. It had a scoter look to it but it was hard to see until it got closer. Sure enough, the slight bank it took gave up the white patch on its wings, a White-Wing Scoter. By the time it had reached the edge of the spread you could see the bright colored beak, it was a drake. Jason pulled up and shot him right in the face as he set. Down he went and dove on impact with the water. We both jumped up and ran straight to the waters edge for a cripple shot. My gun was long empty so I had to throw a shell in just in case he needed help. We waited and waited for him to surface, not uncommon when scoter hunting. I thought I was going to have to go get the boat. Before I could move, up he came, dead. He had just enough energy to dive and that was it. I put my arm around my brother and congratulated him on a job well done. He had done it. He shot Common Goldeneye, Barrows Goldeneye, Greater Scaup, Wigeon, Gadwall, Mallard, and a White-Wing Scoter, all drakes. Not only was this a great accomplishment, but it was also quite a wide variety of birds.

We were now starting to feel the hunger pangs and quickly picked up. Our curiosity of how the Drewry brothers had fared was quickly satisfied. As we came around the bend to the launch we could see their birds lined up on a drift log ready for pictures. Jason put the motor in neutral so we could contain our laughter; they had shot all of two species. On the log were two beautiful limits of drake Surf Scoters finished out with three Barrows Goldeneyes apiece. My suspicions were correct, there was no way they were waiting out different species. Their quick, chaotic shots had given them away.

"Ahhh, the Drewry's, patience of the saints!" I yelled to them. "Now we know who runs the waters out here!"

This was greeted with the universal sign for "whoopdeedoo" sending Jason and me into a fit of laughter. We got to the dock and exchanged all the stories of the mornings hunt. I took out all our birds and laid them beside theirs for some really neat pictures. Not that often you get that many nicely plumed birds together with that kind of variety.

We got all cleaned up and organized, and headed off to lunch. Toby's is a fine tradition for us, and we couldn't wait to dig into those fresh mussels and buffalo burgers. It is located in an area not known for a love of duck hunters, but we have stayed loyal so long now that they don't even mind when we wear our chest wader's right into the restaurant. They even greet us by name, our very own Cheers.

"So how long until you guys gave in and started shooting all those Surfs?" I just had to ask.

"Hahaha, about five minutes!" Bill piped in.

"I knew you guys couldn't turn down all those flocks. You should have seen Jason, he was on a mission. If that White-Wing hadn't of come in we would still be there for sure." I had to brag up my brother a bit. "And now we get a free lunch!"

Just as I said that Bill and Dave just looked at each other and laughed. I knew then it was all a ruse. They had never intended to wait on species and this was all a trick to pick up the tab.

"Oh man, I should have known better, you guys stink . . ." I just smiled and shook my head. When two guys will go to that depth to pick up lunch, you know you have good friends. This certainly raises the bar.

Dang Drewry's.

Chapter 9

Teal Hunting Samish Bay Style

When ever you talk to any old time Waterfowler, or for that matter anyone that considers himself more than a part time weekend warrior, there is one thing they all have in common. This is a home base of water. Be it a lake, a river, a bay, or even a favorite pond or marsh, there is always that spot that the person becomes synonymous with. I can't think of Ben Welton or David Hagerbaumer without thinking of Padilla Bay. Bring up the California legend Bill Pinches, I immediately draw on Humboldt Bay. Jeff Coats? Easy, Chesapeake Bay. Locally we have the Snake River, with Gary March. And Captain Dave? Well, since he refuses to let anyone know where he hunts, I should leave him out of the conversation, but I think you get my point. What do folks think about when it comes to me and my brother? I would hope to think it may be a bit tricky considering all the different areas we hunt, but I know it isn't. Our soul belongs to Samish Bay, and if you asked them, those close to us would nod their head in agreement.

The very first week I got my drivers license I began to drive up there and hunt. Samish is now littered with private clubs, private boat launches, and private everything else, but back then they used to have a huge barley field right off the dike open to public hunting. Jason and I cut our teeth outsmarting ducks there, and more often than not, outsmarting other hunters who at times were more the competition than anything else. The moment the WDFW moved their public access we maintained the area for ourselves by immediately befriending the local farmers. Farm by farm they sold out to clubs, except one. This particular farmer refused to let anyone dictate what happened on his property, and this played into our advantage. We didn't want to plant crops, dig pits, or anything of that nature. That was music to his ears and we were exactly the type of people he wanted to trust with his property. To this day we still maintain that friendship and enjoy some of the best hunts money can't buy. We call it Jim's Farm, or Jimmy's. Eventually we did end up joining a lease nearby, but more for an access to a boat launch. It also gained us access to the famed Brant blinds that can be seen in the middle of the bay on a clear day. At the time of my writing this we still have not enjoyed a hunt in those rickety old stilt blinds, but the plan is there just so we can enjoy some of the history of the area.

When asked about Samish Bay we always say there are two duck seasons, the Teal season and the Pintail season. Sure, there are lots of other species around, and often very plentiful, but those two species are the dominate waterfowl of the area. Early season the Teal seem to swarm up like bees, flocks that number in the thousands. Mostly Green Wings, but we have shot the occasional Cinnamon and Blue Wing. Come mid November the Pintail move in and never leave. During the years that the Pintail seasons were either closed or segmented, most spots would almost become unhuntable. The Pintail flocks are so numerous and plentiful a responsible shot at anything else could not be taken. The Green Wing though, is King of the Samish to us. This is our favorite duck to eat, other than Canvasback. They are such a worthy challenge when on the wing, that this hunt is one we welcome again and again.

The early season days are chosen by a couple of factors. The area we hunt is a pickle grass marsh that comes off a long mud flat and is affected by large tides. To be most effective we need at least a seven foot tide. And of course it would be preferential if it were like this at first light. Throw in a nice light breeze from the south, and we are in business.

We found ourselves with just such conditions on this late October day. We arrived about an hour before sunrise and got to work. The hike is about three hundred yards, just long enough to use our plastic decoys instead of cork or cedar. Not that we don't occasionally hunt the handcrafts here, but it is our philosophy that puddle duck hunting should be as easy as possible. Any time there is a hike involved, go light. Leave the hard work for the divers, they deserve it. Puddler hunting should be like taking a vacation. The hardest job this morning was building the blind. At this spot we don't like to have a permanent blind, so we make one out of scratch for every hunt. This is always an easy task as there are plenty of sticks and long grasses as well as lot of big rocks to build it around.

When we were done tooling around in the pickle grass we set the dekes. The spread we use for Teal is a bag of Avery plastics, six each on the Green Wings, Cinnamons, and the Blue Wings. We keep this bag with us on every hunt we go on during the season. This is our back up plan to our back up plan. If all else fails weather wise, you can always go up to Samish and hunt Teal. It takes only minutes to deploy and just like that you are ready.

The normal habit of the Teal here is to flock up in small groups and work the waters edge up and down the bay. It actually works in our favor if all the clubs have hunters utilizing the blinds, this keeps the birds moving and working. At first light we heard a blaze of gunfire. I looked over at Jason and smiled, we knew the birds would be coming.

The first half hour was pretty dull. The bay was calm and the only birds in the air were crows that seemed extremely high up. We only knew they were there because of their constant cawing. I was just hoping to not see the sea gulls fly. Jason holds a superstition that if flocks of seagull are in the air at first light the ducks will not come. I always laugh at him when he claims this, but it seems to hold true on just about every occasion. But so far so good, as there were no gulls. But there were no Teal either. The guns at the clubs were also silent.

"Is that a live bird?" I heard Jason ask.

I looked at the spread and noticed a single young drake Green Wing had snuck in and was swimming around. We watched him for about five minutes until I couldn't take it any more. I got up and walked to the edge of the water. He sprang into the air and I raised my gun to complete the jump shoot but I didn't pull the trigger. It just didn't feel right.

"Hey, what gives?"

"I don't know, just seemed a bit too easy. He fooled us coming in, I figure I owed it to him," I tried to explain; "You know what I mean?"

"No, all I saw was his breast on my barbeque. Did you come to hunt or do you want to borrow my binoculars, Sally?" This time he was laughing. Not with me, but at me. I gave a quick chuckle and sat down again.

"You know what, your right, I at least should have let you take him," I replied trying to save a little face.

"I'm just yanking you, I wouldn't have shot it either," he said as he looked out over the bay. After a pause, he exclaimed "Nah, I definitely would have shot it."

"Whatever!" These are the types of conversations we have when nothing is flying.

Thankfully there were still no gulls flying either. It was about 9:00 when finally a little action came our way. A pair of Green Wings rifled just out of range and landed about a hundred yards down the beach. Soon after another pair came by and we watched as they swam around and began to feed in the shallows. I knew if more birds were to fly in they would now head straight for these live birds versus our decoys. You just can't compete with the real deal.

"Hey Jay, I am going to walk over and scare those birds out, be right back."

I got out of our pickle grass blind and headed on over. I brought my gun and thought if they were going to hold tight I would try and salvage this hunt. I got about half way there before they saw me and lifted up. Instead of heading out to the open water they turned and came our way. I took a knee and tried to remain motionless. The four birds at first overshot the spread but hooked left and came right on in. Jason was ready and I could here three shots. I turned and headed back to see one of the pairs lying in the water.

"Nice shooting Jay!" I yelled as I briskly marched my way to the blind.

"Nice bird dogging! I appreciate that," he answered as he retrieved his birds.

This seemed to open up a little more action. A few minutes later another small group of about eight to ten birds followed the tide line right to the decoys. We both unleashed a volley of shots that sent five more birds into the water. Before we could get back into the blind, another trio came swinging by. We didn't have our guns ready and they got away, but it was clear the flight was on.

"John, to your right, a nice single."

I turned and fired dropping the drake right onto the beach. This bird was far and away the nicest of the day up to that point. He only had a few brown feathers running down his back but all the other markings of a mature drake were there. My favorite part of a Green Wing Teal drake is the creamy yellow feathers that make up the rear of the bird. I also like the signature horizontal white stripe that marks the sides of his breast. Of course every drake we pick up we look to see if that stripe is vertical following his tertails instead. For those in the know we are looking for his cousin, the European Green Wing. We have yet to score, but you never stop looking.

Down the bay we could hear the guns that had fell silent shortly after morning gun also began to pick up. That is when it hit me.

"Jay, check the tide book, when is high tide?"

He searched through his bag and pulled it out. "High tide was about twenty minutes ago. Nice call."

That is when it hit him as well. Teal prefer a good falling tide and that is what we had. We knew this and were a little disappointed with ourselves for almost giving up on the day. Some days the Teal will move all day, some you have to be patient. Our patience was now paying off.

The next flock numbered more birds than we had seen all morning. This time the ones and twos had brought reinforcements, there were about fifty birds. As they got near the decoys about half split off and headed out to the open water, and the other half stayed the course. We let out another volley and dropped another four birds. Our fortunes had changed and we were having a ball. Among those birds, three were perfect little drakes.

This wave of Green Wings continued for another hour allowing us to pick up the remaining birds we needed for our limits. Our strict rule of drakes is not in effect when we hunt Green Wings. I can only explain this by the fact that we do not choose to follow drake only for science alone, but mostly because it feels better for us. When it comes to Teal, they all feel good. This makes sense when you realize that our lust for barbeque is not prejudiced, and that the hen tastes just as good as the drakes.

The day was so pleasant and enjoyable we stayed on for another hour to enjoy the marsh. When we finally walked out I did what I always do when leaving the Samish. I whisper a little thank you under my breath and take a little bow when I reach the dike. Samish Bay, she always takes care of us Otto boys.

Chapter 10

Ringnecks and Ice on Emery's Ponds

The incoming cold front had us fumbling for a strategy. Too many options at times can really get you second guessing. A temperature drop like this doesn't come around all too often in Washington, and we needed to take full advantage. We were in the third day in a row of lows in the 20's at night with highs in the mid 30's during the day. This meant a lot of the ponds and lakes are already frozen. Our salt water spots can be hit or miss, at times the cold drives birds to the fields to feed. This meant we should also be scouting anything on land. What to do, where to go, these are the fun questions routinely asked by most waterfowl hunters.

Jason suggested we simply take an afternoon drive, and scout all our options for the morning. We both were off work with a few hours of daylight left, this is perfect for scouting, but sacrifices any type of evening hunt. This can be worth it, as a good scouting trip may set you up for a few days, even a week. We got out our trusty old map book and starting plotting our course. We looked at all the spots we had access too, even old ones we hadn't seen in a while. You just never know.

First up was a little farm near Stanwood we called Wood-Teal Way. A few years back Jason had taken a nice drake Wood Duck with a limit of Teal, thus the name. Not much water, only a ditch that widened at the middle creating a small pond that was certainly frozen. The appeal of this farm is the wheat fields and the cut corn. We pulled into the dirt road that we have access to and scoured the place from end to end. There was nothing.

Up next was a cattle farm we called Emery's. I had worked there in my youth and know it well. I grew up in a town just north of Marysville called Lakewood that is only about ten miles from Silvana, where this farm is located. My mother used to drop me off in the mornings and pick me up after she got off work in the evenings. I worked there for three years, from 11 to 13 years old, for all of two dollars an hour. It was hard labor, shoveling manure, painting the barns, and milking cows. You name it, I did it. As an added benefit, however, my labor did earn us lifetime passage to hunt there, and we take advantage of this several times a year. Emery's is definitely a hot or cold type of place, though; you have to hit it just right.

We drove down the gravel road that would take us to the end of the property where two ponds are located. The ponds are surrounded by trees on the west end and have open pasture bordering the east. The gravel road used to drive around the property separated the two bodies of water. The trees make the ponds an ideal hunting spot; you can hide your blind in the thicket and be overlooking a clear shooting lane. They are pretty good size as well, each are equally about a half acre and shallow. You cannot see the ponds until you get to the edge of the trees.

Jason stopped his truck well before we reached the two ponds. We would walk in from here, if there were any birds using the area we didn't want to disturb them. I decided to check the north pond, and Jason went south. I peered through the trees to find nothing but ice. Discouraged, I walked back to the truck. When I got there I found Jason with a look on his face that I had seen before, one I was hesitant to ask about.

"What's up?" I asked inquisitively. The way he was looking had my imagination running wild.

"Get over here, your not going to believe this!"

We immediately darted together towards the south pond. The trees allowed us to get rather close without being detected. What I saw next I can only imagine would have been a turn of the century market gunners dream. Everything was frozen up except for a patch of water that was about twenty yards wide by twenty yards deep. This was created by the spring that feeds the ponds. "Sweet water" as it is called. In this small space were about a thousand Ringneck Ducks. There were so many swirling and squirming around that it reminded me of an ant hill run amok. I stood there transfixed. Jason literally had to grab the back of my shirt and pull me back to the truck.

The scouting trip was over. We jumped into the rig and quickly ran home to prepare for the following morning. Ringnecks are among my favorite ducks to hunt and we call them the "jets" of the waterfowl world. The way they scream into a rig of decoys with reckless abandon gives chills to those lucky enough to have this experience. Neither of us had a full Ringneck cork rig so we had to cheat a bit and use our Scaup and Cans. The only Ringneck decoy I have was carved the year before and I couldn't wait to get it into the water. This was a perfect hunt for its maiden voyage. Jason on the other hand had carved a few, but had given them all away on trade deals or donations. He was wishing he had a few of those back.

The next morning we couldn't get there fast enough. We had to break a path in the ice to get to the "sweet water" that was only about fifteen yards from where we made our blind in the trees. This was perfect. Ruddy made the first trail and I banged out another. The best sign was the fact the Ringnecks were not there in the dark when we arrived. They were not using this for a roost and would for sure be back. I only set a dozen decoys. The space seemed so small I didn't want to crowd it. That seemed kind of funny considering how many birds were there the day before. Still, you go with what you feel is right, and then run with it. I placed my corker in dead center. Jason just shook his head while looking over the dekes. I know what he is going to carve in the off season!

The first half hour after sunrise was completely uneventful. The sky was completely cloudless, and it was cold, really cold. I enjoy watching my breath as I looked around and see nothing but frost and ice. I could see little ice crystals forming on Ruddy's whiskers, but she didn't even notice them. She was too busy watching the sky for wings. Normally it would be a nice and quiet morning but a farmer down the way was running a tractor of some sort. It was slightly distracting and sort of took away the feel of being immersed in the wilderness. The truth is we weren't. We were hunting in the middle of people's livelihoods, a common situation while out in the field.

The first bird to light the decoys was a hen Mallard. She sort of slid in the back door as you would say. I didn't even see her until I heard the water splash. Jason flinched when he heard it, and just smirked as he lowered his arms. She was completely unaware of our presence and continued to preen her feathers and swim with the fakers. Next came a bird flying in low. We crouched down in anticipation but this time we quickly could tell it was another hen, back at ease. The bird circled once and dumped into the pond. This time it wasn't a Mallard, but a hen Canvasback. I was really surprised for in all the years hunting there I had never seen a Can. All I could think was why she wasn't a drake! She joined right in with the Mallard and began to preen away.

Then it happened, out of no where. A flock of Ringnecks, thirty strong, dropped directly into the dekes. No warning, no circling, just a bunch of jets screaming into the water. I stood up out of excitement and the whole flock flushed. I picked two drakes that were bolting to the right and shot in their direction, knocking them both down onto the ice. The rest were too tight to shoot. Jason pulled up and swung on a nice drake lifting high on the left, dropping him on the ice and sliding him thirty feet. Three birds down. I looked over at the decoys to see the Canvasback hen still sitting there with her neck outstretched. The thoughts that must have been going through her mind! She finally picked up as Ruddy began cutting more ice trails to retrieve our birds.

Back in the blind I examined our quarry. All three were perfect drakes. The first thing I look for in a fully matured Ringneck is the actual chestnut brown ring that forms around its black neck. Sure enough, all three had it. I ran my fingers through the feathers on the top of their heads to stand up the crest that gives the bird its shape. The bodies are stark black and white with a perfect mix of gray in the flanks. I started thinking of the feast we were going to have. Ringnecks are a direct cousin to the Canvasback, and taste similar, very good eating indeed.

The new trails Ruddy had made in the sweet water gave the impression of being full of broken glass as the chunks of ice filled the open water. I waded out to kick some of the ice out, when I heard it again. The screaming little jets were coming back. This time they had reinforcements as there were at least fifty circling. I quickly jumped back into the blind. The Ringnecks seemed not to care. Surely they had seen me; they just had to in that spot. As they descended I picked out a nice fat drake that was lower than the rest. My shot sent the flock skyward, and the drake downward. Jason cracked off two shots this time and dropped only one, falling a few feet from mine. Before he could send Ruddy, the flock came back.

I was not ready for this, but Jason was. He sent another one down to the ice about fifteen yards out. That shot would surely send the flock packing, I thought. Nope, they came back again. It seemed they had no where else to go. There probably weren't too many sources of open water in the area and they panicked. This time I was ready. As they lit into the decoys I picked out two more drakes and sent them into the sweet water. Jason managed another shot and one went to the ice. The birds had enough and finally left the area. But not before we were able to shoot six perfect drakes. I have seen this before, hunting Ruddy Ducks on Lake Lenore in Eastern Washington a few years back. A panicked flock with few options basically has to be forced to find a new area.

Ruddy was in retrieving heaven. She had cleanly picked up all the birds and we were hunting again. I was grinning ear to ear with excitement. The fast pace of the action had really gotten the blood flowing. Couple that with the fact we were shooting Ringnecks at a blistering pace and this was about as good as it gets. All the shooting must have alarmed a flock of Trumpeter Swans that had been grazing in a nearby field. They got up and flew directly our way, just yards above our heads. The heavy wing beats and the overall size of the bird is simply amazing. We could see two that were banded. The red of the neck band really stands out on a white bird, especially at close range. We knew of the study rather well, having friends that were participating in it. Seeing their handy work was a small thrill.

About a half hour went by before the next bird would come circling. This was obviously a puddle duck and Jason started giving him a few calls. As soon as he got close enough to identify I knew I wanted this bird. He looked to be a full colored Shoveler drake, a hard bird to come by in Washington. Most Shovelers are long south by now and we have to usually resign ourselves to shooting brown ones early in the season. I waited for him to reach about twenty yards out before I sent him packing into the water. Upon closer inspection I would say he was about two-thirds to full plumage, close enough to be excited about.

I would later regret taking that Shoveler. About an hour after I took him we were barraged by another strong flock of Ringnecks, enabling us to finish out our limits. It is not often we get such a great shoot on all drake Ringnecks and the Shoveler really blew our picture opportunity. None the less, the sweet water in the ice enabled us to have a wonderful day, one I won't soon forget.

Later that night we called Dad and had him over to my house for a nicely prepared feast. I bacon wrapped the breasts of the Ringnecks after stuffing them with jalapeño peppers and onions. After that I barbequed them with our special sauce and served them with some wild rice. Our Dad is a hardened "Mallard only" guy when it comes to ducks on the barbeque, until of course he tried this and admitted it was some of the best waterfowl he had ever eaten. It was a fitting close to a great day.

I ended up shipping my now experienced Ringneck decoy as a gift to Spencer, Captain Dave's oldest son. He needed it for a youth hunt in the Brewster area, where they predominately hunt Ringnecks. This is a much better home, and I am happy the decoy will help create memories for years to come. We have yet to carve a Ringneck spread, but hey, you can't meet every goal at once. It's simply one more thing for us to look forward to doing.

Chapter 11

A Daughters First, a Dogs Last

  It sure felt good to sleep in, even if it was only an extra hour. It was Sunday and I was taking the family to church. After the hunt the day before, Jason and I decided to take a day off. It was a rough one. We were open water Scoter hunting on Skagit Bay. The morning had started off smoothly enough. The waters were calm, the flights were good. In the last leg of the hunt a southern wind kicked up out of points unknown, and the water changed on a dime. In no time we were fighting two to three foot chop. We got out of there before the big storm hit, but any sea faring person will tell you it can take a lot out of you. The weather today called for some of the same winds so we thought we would just wait it out, and take a well deserved break.
  All through church I would look out the clear parts of the stained glass windows and watch the wind blowing on the shrubs in violent frenzies. I kept thinking how nice and relaxing it was to be sitting in church instead of the bow of a boat getting showered with the numbing sea spray. The cushioned pews felt good on my back side. Much better than the cold aluminum seat I would be bouncing off of if we were hitting three footer's at 20 mph. As I listened to the rain pounding on the roof outside, I reflected on how nice it was to be here, completely dry. This was a great break.
  As the sermon progressed, I was having a hard time focusing. My mind kept drifting outside. Break . . . who was I kidding? I didn't want a break.

This wasn't fair to the pastor who was speaking, I realized. I made a better effort to listen. Dr. Tom Albright is a great guy and an excellent speaker. I truly appreciate our church. More importantly, I really enjoy and genuinely respect our Pastor Tom. He knows my attendance is a bit spotty during the waterfowl season. Even though he won't come out and say it, I am sure he understands. He is an avid fly fisherman and outdoorsman as well, and an extremely talented photographer. He knows of the outdoor call, the urge to be immersed in nature. I believe this gift is God given.

So instead of fighting this urge I choose to embrace it. We have talked about this many times. His thoughts and attitudes about being in the great outdoors are one of the reasons I like him so much. I once told him of my pact with God. I promised God a long time ago that every time I witness a beautiful golden sunrise, a majestic white covered mountain illuminated by the sunlight, or the soft glistening of low light over wind swept waters, that I would say a little thank you prayer. Thanks for creating such a bounty of beauty. Even on the days where the wind cuts through you like a knife, or the rain hits you so hard in the face it stings, I say this prayer. This is my personal church, and the flying birds are my congregation. Pastor Tom gave me a little smile and patted my back. Like I said, I think he understands. That or he respects my justification. Either way, it makes me happy.

Toni could tell I was getting a little antsy. She leaned over and whispered in my ear, "John, after the service why don't you call your brother and try to squeeze in an afternoon hunt." And that is why I love her so much.

When the congregation was released I hurried to get my youngest daughter Kaden out of Sunday school. I could feel the coy smirk Toni was giving me on the back of my neck as I quickly bustled along, but hey, now time was of importance. After I grabbed her I made my way back to the front door where Toni, my oldest daughter Haley, and my middle daughter Abi were waiting. I was about to make a clean break, when right before me moved Pastor Tom.

"Good to see you John. But I have to ask, what are you doing here today with winds like this?"

I couldn't believe he was asking me this. This hit me by surprise and reaffirmed my opinion of him. With the biggest smile I could muster I answered, "The "thank you's" to God only go so far, every once in a while he needs to see me with slacks on!" I didn't dare tell him I was trying to hustle my way to a marsh as we spoke.

He smiled, shook his head a little, and replied, "Well, don't let me hold you up."

There was no fooling him. This guy has me figured out.

The moment I got to our truck I called Jason. There was no answer. I just kept on hustling. We only live five minutes from our church, and that is if the only stop light on the way turns red. I tried him again as we entered the driveway, and this time he answered.

"Hey, what's up?"

"Jay, I know we were taking a break today, but I changed my mind, let's go!"

"Oh man, I wished you would have called about a half hour ago. I'm on my way to Lynnwood to be with the family for lunch. I can't make it." I could tell there was some disgust in his voice for us even pondering a break anyhow. Now it was too late for him and I was on my own.

When it comes to our families and hunting we have worked out a very structured plan that has worked for many years. Both Jason and I were dedicated hardcore hunters before we met our wives and we were very upfront about this from the start. The last thing we want for our wives is for them to become "duck widows" during the season so we have come up with a balance that we do our best to follow. All of our hunts, excluding special occasions or those we have to travel for, are done by 11:00 am. That usually gets us home by noon and we spend the rest of the day with the family. We are also both very fortunate that we have jobs that lend a certain amount of flexibility. I can partly work from home some days and often do so during the season. All this contributes to the fact that I see my wife more than the average Joe. So much so that there are even times she is kicking my butt out the door.

"Jason can't go? Sorry about that, I can tell you were going crazy in church today," Said Toni, as she placed her hand on my arm.

"That's O.K., today will be a nice break." There was that break word again. She knew I wouldn't go alone. When I was younger I wouldn't have thought twice about going solo. It just seems the older I get the more I would rather share the hunt. I suppose I am getting soft.

"Dad, can you take me today?"

I couldn't believe it. My oldest daughter Haley had just asked if she could go. This was certainly a first and it hit me totally by surprise. My daughters are girly girls and they have never showed all that much interest in hunting. I am fine with that and have long since accepted that they would rather go shopping, or really anything else. I wasn't going to let this opportunity go and I jumped all over it.

"Really? Seriously? That's great! I am sure I have plenty of extra clothes and I know my old chest waders cinched in the right places will fit you close enough. Let's go get changed and get out of here!"

"There is one condition though." Here it comes, I thought. I was going to have to promise to take her to the mall afterwards, get her nails done, maybe something even worse. She paused, "We have to take Comet. I have never seen her hunt and I want to see her in action before it is too late."

This ripped through me like a lightening bolt. My first reaction was one of pride that she would think of something like this. My second was one of worry. I had taken Comet on a grouse hunt earlier in the season and this was to be her final hunt, her last before her retirement. It took days of lying around to recover from this hunt and I wasn't sure if she had enough in her. I had to make it work though, how could I turn Haley and her request down?

"Sure, let's do it. We have to go easy on her, but I think it will be O.K."

I ran upstairs to change my clothes and to dig out some old shirts for Haley to wear. I started drifting off on memories of Comet and what this hunt would now entail. Haley was born the same week as Comet, twelve years earlier. I remember driving to the farm where I purchased Comet. Haley, being an infant, rode in the back of the car in her child seat. I put my new puppy in a box for the ride home and she started whining. This got Haley crying. I remember thinking that my life only a month prior was quiet and organized. That drive home with both of them screaming at the top of their lungs symbolized my future, and how much life had changed. The two would grow up together and create quite a bond. Even their names are linked, Haley's Comet.

After getting Haley outfitted and ready to go, I went to the backyard to get my old dog. She was lying on the deck fast asleep. I woke her by petting her. Calling was pointless, as she is now completely deaf. Surprisingly she sprang onto her feet and followed me out to the truck where her kennel awaited. I lifted her up and placed her inside. Haley came over and loved her up, which gave Comet even more perkiness. I could tell I was in for some fun.

I decided the easiest and closest hunt would be a small little cove on the north end of our property on Samish Bay. It normally doesn't hold a lot of ducks this early in the season, but I could drive right up to the beach and drop everything off. That way there would be no hike and in case anything happened to Comet I would quickly be able to get her out of there. The water was also very shallow on the tide that day. I could walk out 500 yards in the mud flat and still never go deeper than my waist. My goal was to shoot at least one bird for her to retrieve. That way Haley would get to see her in action. Haley still hadn't taken the Hunters Ed classes and would only be watching. This was O.K. with me. I was a bit worried about the fact she had never seen anything die before. I wasn't quite sure how she was going to handle seeing a duck get shot. It thought it better for her to experience this before she does it for herself. The last thing I wanted was for her to be completely turned off of hunting before she even got started.

On the way there, we talked and talked. It is amazing the conversations you can have with a twelve year old when you find yourself doing something that puts you on an even level. I could tell she was enjoying the one on one time and there were no other sisters there to bug her or interrupt her trains of thought. We began to reflect on all the good times we had with Comet, and how funny she had gotten in her old age. Comet really does act like an old lady. Her face can simultaneously give the impression of wisdom and of being bothered at the same time. I love that. Losing her was going to be a life lesson for Haley. I wanted this impromptu hunt to be a day she thinks back on with a smile when she remembers her little Comet.

I drove the truck right down to the edge of the bay. There were about twenty or so Pintails and Green Wing Teal milling around in the shallows that immediately erupted and headed to the safety of the big water. I looked over at Haley and her eyes were as large as saucers.

"It's pretty cool to see ducks while you are hunting instead of at a park! It's so different."

"No kidding, now lets hope they come back," I replied. "Hopefully they saw your pretty little face and want another look."

"Whatever Dad, you're a dork." She smiled as she said this.

We got out and I walked her down to where we were going to set up. The beach was made up of old oyster shells embedded into the sand and mud that was slowly eroding back into the bay. This created a sort of shelf of about three feet high a short distance from the water. This was a perfect place to sit comfortably and, with little effort, get somewhat hidden. I placed a small camouflaged chair right at the edge for her.

"Would you mind if I set out the decoys?" She asked.

"Sure, I'll get Comet. Do you remember how the ducks were sitting and feeding when we pulled in? Place them in the water and try to copy how that looked."

I dropped off the bag of decoys by the water and she went to work. When I got to the truck I could hear Comet ferociously licking the door of her kennel, a sign she was ready to go. This was a common thing for her to do, and it sounds just nasty. It would always drive Jason nuts. Through the years I would tell him that I would try and train her not to lick like that but I never did anything about it. I kind of liked watching how it bugged Jay. He is going to kill me when he reads this.

As soon as I opened the door she bolted out and jumped on her own to the ground. I winced and was upset with myself for not grabbing her first. It did not seem to matter. She immediately ran to Haley's side, sat, and patiently waited while the decoys were being thrown into the water. If Haley moved to her right a step, Comet would heel herself again and sit in perfect obedience.

"Wow, Dad, Comet is so well trained! I can't believe how she is just sitting here by me while I do this? This is awesome!"

"Uh, yeah . . . perfectly trained . . ." I said with a half smile of amazement. I couldn't believe it. The last couple of years in the field would have made Richard Wolters grimace in pain if he could have seen her. In her youth I spent a lot of time training and she was a great asset in the field. As she went deaf and got older I stopped reinforcing certain habits and it usually showed. I figured it was better to put up with a few annoying missteps than to be constantly yelling at a dog who stopped listening. I was expecting to have to practically chain her to the truck so she wouldn't be frolicking around in the water. Instead she was acting like Tar in her prime, and how she used to work for me when I was with my Dad. She looked good too. Her coat was shining, her ears perked in excitement. And there she was, sitting besides Haley thinking she was three years old again. I stared at that image and made a mental picture, I never want to forget that moment.

After we got settled, and the gear was organized, I asked her, "Haley, do you want to run Comet on the retrieves?"

"Yes, I was going to ask you if I could. I know what to do, Grandpa John taught me." she replied, rather confidently. "Heel Comet!"

Comet whisked around and actually heeled to Haley while she was sitting in her chair. All I could think was "who is this dog, and what have you done with Comet!"

"Hey, if Grandpa showed you, than you probably know more than me."

It took about fifteen minutes of relaxing and watching before our first duck started to work. I pulled out my call and gave it a few quacks pulling the little Green Wing hen to about sixty yards out. She then flared away as fast as she had approached. We weren't hidden really well and I knew it would be a tough hunt.

"Uncle Jason was right; you ARE really bad with that call!" She started laughing hysterically.

"What? And you could do better?" I started laughing too. But I did make a mental note to yell at Jason later.

"Can I try?"

"Sure, let me see what I have in here," I said as I started digging through my ammo bag. I keep a few calls on me and I knew I should have a good double reed for her to play around with.

"Ah, here you go, and you can have it." I reached over and gave her a nice little Primos call that would be perfect for her to practice with. "Let's see what you got."

"Thanks! Uncle Jason taught me to blow "tucka, tucka, tucka" for a hen Mallard feeding call, how is this?" She put it to her mouth and called away. My first thought was how good she really sounded. My second was holy cow, first my Dad is teaching her how to train dogs and my brother is teaching her how to call ducks? Where the heck was I when all this training went down?

"Haley, that is really good! The next duck I want you to call just like that. And by the way, make sure you tell Dad and Jason that I taught you how to set those decoys, O.K.?"

"Uh, Dad, Uncle Jason already told me about that too!"

Before I could take any more abuse, a flock of Pintail was in the air and coming towards our spread. Perfect timing, I was getting beat up pretty bad.

"Haley," I whispered, "go ahead and give them your feeding call nice and soft, and as they get close go softer and softer until they commit. Then just stop."

I watched the flock fly right to the edge of the bay about a hundred yards down and slowly work their way on the tide line in our direction. I glanced over and saw her staring up with her eyes wide as her call got softer and softer. I looked down at Comet and she was matching Haley's sight direction. It was poetry. The calling stopped. I looked up to see the flock of about ten setting right on us. I pulled up and sifted through the birds looking for the best drake I could find. When I found him I waited for the Sprig to separate from the others and pulled the trigger.

"You got him!"

The big bull Sprig folded and fell cleanly dead into the water. I immediately looked over at Haley to get her reaction. The smile on her face told me everything I needed to know. The biggest surprise of all was that Comet was still at heel. I could lie and say I expected this, but an honor dog Comet was not.

"Back!" At Haley's call the old gal sprang into action. The Pintail was about twenty yards out and floating face down. When Comet got there, it was still too shallow for her to swim and she was basically wading in the water. It was perfect. The walk back was slow and deliberate and when she got to shore she dropped the bird at the edge and slowly shook the water from her coat. I actually felt good about that. Had she brought it all the way back to hand I would have been certain this was not my dog. I laughed under my breath as I picked up the bird and thought how funny it would be if I took her over to my Dad's for a little force fetching reinforcement.

"Thanks Dad, that is what I wanted to see. I have always heard how awesome Comet was at retrieving and now I can say that I know." She walked over to her and proceeded to give the dog a big hug, wet fur and all.

"Nice job calling them in! That sounded really good." I said as I put my arm around her shoulders.

"Think so? I will have to tell Uncle Jason I showed you how it's done."

After that we sat and talked and admired the harvested Pintail for awhile. For the first time she really paid attention to the different colors and the hues of the plumage. A bird is much different in hand compared to pictures. I taught her all about the tertails, scapulars, the speculum, and all the other feather groups that I could remember. I tried not to bore her with all the scientific descriptions but her current goal in life is to be a Marine Biologist, so I figured she would be interested, and she was.

We ended up picking up a nice little pair of Green Wing Teal about an hour later and decided to call it a hunt. The early energy Comet had shown had worn off. I was really satisfied that I got one more day in field with her and I couldn't have asked for a better situation. On the way home we stopped by Grandpa John's house and then we went to Jason's so we could show off the birds. And more importantly for Haley, she could let them see her in camo. The day had started out simple enough and ended as one I will never forget. Comet passed away the next spring; the very same month that Haley took her Hunters Education course. She passed with a perfect score. Thanks to this last hunt I will forever have a memory that serves as a capstone to Comet's journey. Hers was a life of love and service to her family, my little Haley's Comet.

Chapter 12

Marina Mallards

    The one thing that separates Washington State from other areas is our true variety in waterfowl. Where else can you make it a goal to shoot 25 different species in a given season? Also add that they can be shot in the finest of winter plumage? With all this abundance of diversity an outsider would probably think the Barrows Goldeneye's are chased mercilessly, or that every hunter has a Harlequin on the wall. Nothing could be further from the truth. Every year an estimated 150,000 people here rush out to their local sporting goods store and buy their hunting license. Of that number, only about 950 will apply for the free Sea Duck Harvest card. Only a few more will care enough to take the time to send in for the Brant Card. After that only about a third will actually hunt them, even less on the Brant. Of that third, a majority is made up of out of state hunters looking to collect a trophy. What about the other birds? The Common Goldeneye, Hooded Merganser, Ringneck, Ruddy Duck, Lesser Scaup, Greater Scaup, just to name a few, go largely ignored. Not that I am complaining, or heck, even trying to recruit too many new people, but I am continually amazed that more people don't take advantage of what is right under their noses.

For a few years in the early and mid 90's, Jason and I toured with a collection of waterfowl mounts to various Ducks Unlimited events, Washington Waterfowl Association seminars, even some church fund raising wild meat feed shows. Basically anywhere there was an interest in ducks. The collection had all the legally hunted species of waterfowl found in North America, all 32 birds, lined up on shelves for some up close viewing. At these events we would ask people to identify all the birds on a tally sheet of paper. When the event was over we would take all the sheets that had at least 20 correct into a bucket and pull out a winner who would get some sort of prize. I ended up donating the entire collection to the WWA, and they continue to travel with the collection to this very day, conducting the same tests. It is a great way to educate hunters and bird watchers on identification. Most had never seen some of the birds and were shocked to hear that the majority were harvested in their home state.

What began to concern us was the total lack of ID skills the average hunter possessed. Of the thousands of sheets we collected and saved, the average amount of correct answers was a measly five right. That is downright scary when you consider the tight regulations on some species. You should have seen some of the guesses. My personal favorite was a fellow, who after just bragging he had shot most of them, guessed Greater Cinnamon Teal for a Gadwall. Another once called the Common Goldeneye a Greater Bufflehead. It was hard to keep a straight face when I told them of their errors. We have turned that lack of knowledge into a personal quest to motivate and educate wherever and whenever we can. After all, as hunters we are always going to be judged by our lowest common denominator. And I really don't want that guy representing me when he shoots too many Pintails thinking they were Wigeon.

What bird did they always get right? The Mallard of course. I can't recall a single sheet where that bird was filled in wrong. In Washington the Mallard is King. There is the attitude here that if it isn't a Mallard, it isn't worth pursuing. I call it the Mallard Mystique. I have come to think 99.9% of the hunters I come across outside of my usual circles feel this way. Every thing else is just a fish duck, or a crap duck. If anything else was "accidentally" shot on their hunts they would always start out by either telling you it was "slow" or they just "wanted to give the dog some work". This all cracks me up of course, and I figure it to be their loss. I mean, this is a hobby and if that is the way they choose to enjoy it who am I to tell them any different. I chalk it up to the old adage "ignorance is bliss" and count my lucky stars I don't have to compete for parking space where I hunt Canvasbacks.

With all of that said I must admit that I enjoy hunting Mallards. I love calling in a big fat Greenhead and getting him to commit to my decoys, or watching a flight of thousands lift off the bay in a wind storm. Jason and I chase them more than we let on, and in most years the Mallard will make up the majority of our harvest. Washington is home to some of the finest Mallard gunning in the lower 48, and that is on both sides of the Cascades. Around mid-November every year we get a huge push from up north and they largely never leave. We also have the luxury of a relatively large local breeding population that keeps us busy until the big boys arrive.

One fact about hunting in Washington is that no matter what you are pursuing, no matter what decoy spread you have out, or even in any condition, you will decoy a Mallard. It doesn't matter if I am hunting Scoters over mussel beds, Oldsquaws in a hundred feet of water, or even Red Breasted Mergansers in a current cut running with bait, a Mallard will descend on my spread. It is the one thing I can always count on. Most will get a free pass if I am in diver mode, but some come in so nice they just have to be taken out of the gene pool. I mean, should a Mallard that thinks an Oldsquaw decoy is part of his family be allowed to propagate? When that happens, I like to think I am helping out the natural selection.

Being in so many different areas also has it advantages for scouting. One of our best Mallard hunting spots is located about five hundred yards away from a beach where we hunt Goldeneyes. After a couple of years of watching them pour into this back bay, we had a "McFly" moment of, hey, we should be hunting those Mallards. The first couple of hunts were just unfair, generations of birds that had never seen hunting pressure. We now rotate this particular spot to only a couple of hunts a year to keep the birds nice and, well, uneducated would be the best word.

The first time we took Captain Dave to this spot he was amazed at how dumb these birds had become. He gave them the nickname of "Marina Mallards", a name that has stuck for many years and I love it. These birds, and most little Mallard population pockets we find in remote areas, act no different than the cross bred mongrels found at the parks or the boat launches. Their lack of common sense makes for some fun gunning. Every time we get done with a Mallard hunt in our traditional spots we comment on how much smarter these birds are and look forward to hitting the Marinas. Of course I personally prefer the dumb ones. They just make me look better. I would call myself an average caller, but these birds make me feel like Robert Strong.

We usually save our Marina Mallard hunts for days we can't get on the big water and want a Plan B. The back bay they use is always calm in any type of wind and the chop on the surrounding water adds to the numbers seeking refuge. This was one of those days. We had 20 to 30 knots out of the south, too rough for most hunts. A perfect day, I thought, and I called Jason the evening prior. He agreed and in the morning we found ourselves packing in to our little out of the way cove.

I would like to say we deployed the optimum strategy in our decoy placement, but that would just be a lie. We simply tossed them as far as we could off the beach and tried to keep them somewhat in a group. At our regular haunts we would take great care to set the perfect rig, or what our version of perfect is, but in all honesty it just didn't matter and we knew it. The next job would normally be to build a blind. Not here. That job is replaced with finding the perfect log to rest on while sitting on the beach. This always shocks the guests we bring here, no blind for Mallards? It doesn't take them long to understand why that would be just wasted effort.

At first light we had birds all over us. It was overcast and gray with strong winds making ID a little difficult. We had to wait for about ten minutes before we could tell what was what. My first bird came in from the left, a lone drake. I missed my first shot and then connected on the second. At the same time Jason shot his first bird and Ruddy was on her way. I decided to walk out and grab my own bird quickly so I could get back to the beach and start hunting again. When I was ankle deep, another drake was locked on the rig. I stood completely still until he was about fifteen yards away. I swung through the setting bird and had number two down. I grabbed both birds and ran back to the beach.

I reloaded my gun and looked up just in time to see three drakes right in front of Jason. He shouldered his gun and his first shot dropped two, a perfect scotch double. His second shot sent the third into a tail spin landing on the beach. I didn't have time to admire the carnage as I had two pair only feet above the water on my side. I shot the first drake just before he landed. This sent the remaining three into the air. I looked down the barrel trying to find the other drake. The hens were in the way and he got away. We had seven, half way there, and only about a half hour had passed.

A small break in the action gave us time to reload and calm down. There is nothing better than the chaos of a hot puddle duck hunt and we were right in the middle of one. I looked over at Jason, who was all smiles. He gave me a quick head nod of confidence then immediately looked up towards the skies.

I quickly turned to see a flock that must have numbered a hundred birds, all locked and loaded on our spread. I picked out the first drake I could see clearly and sent him packing. The flock darted everywhere, confusion had clearly broken out. Some even landed. I noticed a lone Pintail mixed in with about six Mallards trying to sneak out the left corner, my corner. I decided to let the Sprig go and shot the drake Mallard right behind him. This sent the birds that landed into the air, and by a stroke of luck I picked out a drake and shot him as well. I now had three on the water and only needed one more, time to be really selective. I looked back over to Jason who was now on the edge of the water directing Ruddy. He had shot a nice double himself and she was in the process of retrieving them.

"How many do you have left Jay?" I asked trying to bring some organization to our cluster.

"One more to go, you?" He answered, never taking his eye off of Ruddy.

"Same here, only one left!"

As Ruddy finished retrieving all our birds we took a moment to collect ourselves. There was no rush, the birds were still coming. I walked over to Jason to admire his birds, all prime Greenheads. As I was standing there, we had birds landing in the spread. It is moments like this you wish it was always so good. I had to remind myself it was only this feverish because of our lack of pressure, so soak it in and relish the moment. The fact we will wait another month to even consider hunting this place is why these birds are still landing.

Jason decided his next and last bird would only be a single that he himself called in. I respect that, but told him I was going to take the next shot that looked good. It didn't take long, moments later a drake came in from behind, presenting me with a perfect ten yard shot. I was done.

"Jay, to my left!" I looked over to see he was already watching him. He gave a couple of high balls that immediately turned him into our area. Several feeding chuckles and he was locked. In no time he was belly up, a kicking chicken. This time there was no reason to hustle and Jason took his time with Ruddy for her last retrieve of the day.

There is something about a Greenhead limit that gets the soul stirred. Of all the unique trophy hunts we do in a season, we know this one will get the envy of most Washington Waterfowlers. Our version of a stack-em-up tailgate picture is to take all the Mallards and lay them on a nice drift log. Of course we had to sit a while and smoke a few cigars and relive the chaos. I told Jason of the Pintail I could have taken and he told me of the group of Wigeon he passed on. We were both glad we did that, seeing all that green was making the moment pretty special.

I never will fully understand the Mallard Mystique of the Washington Waterfowler. Their absolute snub and total disregard of anything not green, referring to all other ducks as crap or fish ducks. What I do understand is the pride one feels when holding seven Mallards by the feet and calling it a hunting day. The hunt took only one hour, but what an hour it was. I called Captain Dave that afternoon.

"Did you get that out of your system?" He asked, knowing full well what the mallard hunt is all about.

"Yep, I feel much better now."

"Good, now let's go shoot some Bluebills tomorrow and do some real hunting!"

Then there are those that are the opposite, too some the Mallard is the "crap duck". I guess I can respect that too.

Chapter 13

The Mighty Merganser

It was pitch dark, so dark you could barely see your hand in front of your face. The water was calm and the weather was mild. The skies were full of black luminous clouds blocking the nighttime stars. All I could see were the red and green running lights of "Big Grey" as we ran slowly to our beach head destination. It was a long run in some treacherous open waters and Captain Dave was taking his time. My job was to watch for "dead heads" with the spot light, those dangerous stumps or logs floating aimlessly and drifting by the tide. Hitting something like that at full speed will quickly put a damper on the day for sure. Also on the boat with us is Dave Hollingsworth. Dave is a longtime friend of Captain Dave's. He lives on the Olympic Peninsula near

A SEASON OF WING-SHOOTING

the bay we are hunting today. He has been a wing shooter his entire life and on occasion helps Captain Dave guide clients, especially when he has big groups. The reason he was with us this morning is we all have something in common, the love of the Red Breasted Merganser.

It's a little lonely sitting in the bow of the boat on those long dark rides. The solitude gives you time to think. All I could hear was the humming of the four stroke motor and the sound of the waves lapping on the sides of the boat. You can't afford to take your eye off the water for even a second. Every once in a while a sea gull will take flight from his roost and create a wake large enough to cause a momentary alarm of something in the water. After seeing this a few times you get used to it and stop giving the arm signal to go left or right. I kept recollecting all the futile attempts I had hunting the salt Merganser. This is no ordinary bird. When most folks think of a Merganser, they quickly laugh it off as the worst "fish" duck or "crap" duck in the wild. What they don't know, or understand, is what a worthy game bird they really are. I try and explain it this way. Imagine attempting to hunt mallards over a flooded rice field. But when you show up in the morning that rice field has moved, and you can't find it. In its place is just a wide open dirt field, so you set up there. You get skunked so in the afternoon you look for, and find, the rice field again in a completely different spot. The next morning, you show up, and the rice field is moved, again. So goes the Merganser. Their food source is constantly moving, here today, gone tomorrow. Scouting is almost impossible. The only trick you can use is to find a morning or afternoon fly zone to catch them as they move from the roost to there next meal. Only problem is, they break habits quick. Just when you think you have them figured out, they are gone, moved on to another bay.

"Dave, to the left!" I yelled out in vain. He couldn't hear me but saw my arm movements and maneuvered out of the way of the floating log. I felt good I did my job, but I could feel Dave kick the motor down just a touch. Thinking they may be in the water is different than actually seeing something floating. It puts reality back into the equation and gives a little more caution.

Visibility was still no more than ten feet when we reached the first spot. Both Dave's had been watching the Red Breasteds for over a week and they had been using two different flight corridors. Both flocks were feeding in different spots almost every time so we were going to run a little traffic and try to decoy them in the middle of their route. Hollingsworth got out of the boat first.

"I'll hunt this spot alone, why don't you guys run up the spit to the other side and hit 'em there. This way we got them covered," he said while grabbing his gear. It was a good plan, that way we were somewhat mobile. If they were only using one of the areas we could easily join back up.

"Sounds good." Captain Dave handed him the rest of his decoys and we were off to our beach. Having never been there before I was looking forward to seeing something new. I jumped back into the bow and resumed my duties. This leg of the journey took only about ten minutes. I couldn't help but think about Hollingsworth sitting on that beach all by himself. Ten minutes away can be quite far when you are out in the middle of no where. Kind of spooky in the dark, I thought, yet kind of neat.

Our spread of decoys was quite unique. Not too many people have Merganser rigs and I consider mine to be in "just getting started" mode. Eventually I want a dozen or so of each of the three species but right now I have to mix and match. I have a Hooded I carved and also one whittled by Brad Forgey, a carver who hails from the Spokane area. Forgey may just have the largest Merganser rig in the country, his passion for the sawbills spans many years. His recent addition of a half dozen Commons in various courtship positions is truly outstanding. I have to find a way to needle one of those out of him. Joining the rest is a few Engelhardt carved Red Breasteds that both Jason and I own.

Jason couldn't make this hunt, due to work, but I did grab his decoys. He has a really nice Hooded and Red Breasted he carved that I just couldn't leave behind. Rounding out the spread was a few dozen E Allen's that Drewry assembled and painted. Their rendition of Mergansers is spot on and makes the rig look quite realistic. My favorite part about hunting Mergansers is showing the pictures of the spread to those "Mallard only" guys. The look on their faces is truly priceless.

I think my favorite decoy is one of the Engelhardt's. Our first Merganser decoy was a solid cedar Red Breasted carved by Chris for Jason. That decoy ended up on the outskirts of just about every spread we deployed for years before we got serious about having an exclusive Merg rig. The beak is quite thin and has had to be repaired a time or two, but overall it has withstood a lot of abuse and keeps on producing. I love decoys with a history. It went perfect with the decoy he gave us on Opening Day.

By the time the decoys were all placed and we were settled into our makeshift drift wood blind the light was starting to peer over the water. The dark clouds were drifting slowly south and the sun was beginning to peak through. I dug my feet into the sand to get as comfortable as I could and loaded up. I couldn't wait to see the first "RB's" as we called them. They are much different than their cousin the Common Merganser. A bit smaller and certainly sleeker, the RB is one of the most shy and decoy wary of any duck I have ever hunted. I have heard folks say that in some areas they can't get them out of their dekes. Upon further questioning it often boils down to just one hunt where they were most likely lucky to be near a bait source, and had no intention of hunting them that day. Just incidentals birds while hunting for something else. I have never heard of another hunter who specifically targets them have any type of regular consistent success. I know I never have.

For every successful hunt I probably have ten where I give up and try something else. The Common, or Goosander as we like to call them, however is a bit easier to nail down. These clumsy large birds tend to stay in river systems where it is much easier to decoy a flight. We have enjoyed many successful hunts cutting them off as they strolled down the river looking for food. Hooded Mergansers are a completely different story. Our best spots for consistent gunning are salt water beaches close to a fresh water pond or lake. They seem to love trading between the two. Given the fact all three Merganser species tend to prefer such diverse habitat it is quite a challenge to harvest all three in the same day. I have tried a couple of times with no success. Captain Dave is the only person I have ever known to pull this off, and that was with a hen Common in the mix. A "Merganser Slam" of all three being perfect drakes would sure be something to see. To me it is a challenge and I hope to achieve it one day.

An hour drifted by and we hadn't decoyed a thing. Drewry got restless and decided to jump in the boat and do a little scouting. That left me alone on the beach. I could see periodic flights out in the open water scurrying from one spot to another. I knew that was a fool's trip, plenty of times I have set up in a layout only to watch the RB's avoid me like the plague. Another hour went by and I decided to call Hollingsworth on his cell.

"How are you doing over there? I asked. I can't hear anything." There was a land spit and quite a distance between us so not hearing any gun shots would not be out of the question.

"Pretty slow, but I don't care. At first light I nailed a hog! Perfect feathers, he is sweet," he replied with a satisfaction in his voice I was quite jealous of.

"Have you seen more?"

"I could have taken a few hens, but let them pass. Still looking for his brothers."

Before I could answer him I dropped the phone to the ground. A trio of RB's were ripping down the beach and heading my way. I could tell they weren't going to slow down and look at the dekes. It was two juvenile drakes and a young hen. I mounted my gun when they were about eighty yards out and before I knew it the speeding birds were on me. My first shot was clearly behind them. I adjusted on the second and sent the back drake tumbling into the water with his head up. I noticed this and instead of shooting at the other drake I high tailed it to the beach and cleaned up my bird on the water. I quickly ran out to inspect my bird to find he was younger than he seemed in flight. It was a start. I called Hollingsworth back and told him I was in the books with a juvenile drake.

Moments later another pair actually locked on the decoys and in they drifted. This shot was much easier and I sent another young bird tumbling. The only way I could see he was the drake was his size compared to the hen. It takes a couple of years before a Merganser will get his breeding plumage. RB's also are among the last of the ducks to color up in a given year. This all adds to the challenge of getting that trophy drake.

Sitting there with two drakes on the log had me feeling a little better. Captain Dave came back from his scouting mission and suggested we move to another beach he saw some birds shuffling around and we moved. I figure if they are such a mobile bird maybe the key was to do the same. This ate up the rest of the morning and by the time we were resettled it was near noon. I knew we would be in for a long haul.

Our first flock was a good ten birds. Like the birds before, these had no intentions of checking out the spread and were just moving through. I let Dave shoot first and he unloaded. I saw three birds drop before I even pulled up, only allowing myself one shot as they tried to leave. Down came another young drake, and this time I thought I saw some green in his head. I was excited to go check him out but I froze when I heard some wings above and behind me.

"Dave, look up!" Our shooting had spooked a trio of ducks that had been spending the day in the back marsh about a hundred yards behind the beach. I didn't even notice this when we got there and certainly would have thought if there was anything around it would have left while we were setting up. When they reached us they were just twenty yards up. Drewry was already knee deep walking to his dead birds when he turned around and shot at the passing puddlers. Two of the birds came crashing down and I shot clean up and dropped the third. Mine dropped right on the beach in front of me, a perfect drake Gadwall.

"Oh man, I just shot a perfect pair of Gaddies!" Dave yelled, "I have wanted a pair this nice for the office for a long time, sweet!"

Gadwall in hand I made my way for my downed RB. Sure enough he had some green on his head, but still missing any of the long head feathers that make up their trademark look. Getting closer, I thought.

It only took another twenty minutes for Dave to get his last two Mergansers to finish out his limit. Other than the drake Gadwall there was no color. That was O.K., we were looking forward to a big cook out that night and we now had plenty of meat. I would say the second most asked question when folks inquire about hunting Mergansers, after of course the first of "Why?" is "do you eat them?" I love eating Merganser and have a hard time telling the difference between that and a Mallard when pulled right off the barbeque. I have often fooled a few people who dispute that and had them unknowingly eating Merganser. Most times I won't even tell them what I did and keep it to myself for a good chuckle, or maybe it is just the fact I don't want a broken nose. Either way, I rarely defend eating them and chalk it up to the old adage you have to eat what you shoot. If you don't want to eat Merganser, don't shoot one. If you think it is gross, well, you better not eat at my house. You just never know what you might get!

"John, check out that single. Old bull, heading right to us," Dave whispered.

I saw it. My pulse picked up as he neared the set. At first he looked like he was going to skirt around for no shot. Last second, almost like he had a string tied to him circling a pole, he came crashing in. My first shot sent him into a head first dive immediately disappearing. I ran to the edge of the water with my gun at the ready. When he popped up he was about twenty yards to the left. I knew if I didn't make a good quick shot he could be gone just like that. As I pulled up I heard a BANG!

"Sorry John, it's what I do for a living!"

I excitedly started laughing. All season long Captain Dave cleans up crips and is quite good at it. I should have known he wouldn't let that bull get away and that he would beat me to the draw. When I picked him up I saw what I was looking for all day long. He had a perfect green crest resembling flowing hair. The black and white checkered feathers right before the scapulars was full plumed. His eyes were still bright red and glowing. He was a fine specimen and I couldn't contain my joy.

When we picked up Hollingsworth we learned he had shot a nicely plumed Pintail that veered too close to his rig. He also had a few more juvenile RB's. We had quite a brace of birds. That night we feasted like royalty and laughed at how some folks think we are just flat out crazy. I figure it is their loss. To know and respect what a great Merganser hunt can be is only shared among a small group of Waterfowlers, and to me, we are a very lucky group.

Chapter 14

Snow Birds

 The forecast today was for a mix of snow and rain. They were wrong. On the way to our spot this morning we were cutting new trails on the roads in four wheel drive and the snow was coming down so thick that I only had visibility of about twenty yards. The night before we were hoping this would be the case so we decided to get up an extra hour early to have plenty of time to get there. I can honestly say I have never been let down hunting in conditions like this, I knew we were in for a treat.
 When we arrived Jason and I hiked down to the waters edge to get a look at the situation. The distant lights of civilization created a warm glow off the snow in the darkness. Our spot was called a lake but it really was more of a brackish overflow of the bay. Many years ago the dike had broken here and the portion of lands that were flooded was old farm fields. You can still see the

old fence posts sticking out of the water in some places. Early in the season the water is quite low and this makes the lake much easier to hunt. The edge of the lake is full of little islands of wild brush where you can settle in and hide. Later in the season the water rises covering all the natural blinds. That is when we rely on our Pods. We grass them up to match the edge and lay out right in the small boats.

Jason surveyed the area as I stared up into the falling snow. I love the way it hits my face and lands on my tongue. I always feel like a little kid, the feeling of excitement you get when the biggest news of your little life is a canceled school day.

"The water is pretty high so I say we hit the north end."

"Let's do it," I answered him back. I was anxious to get on the water and so was he.

We had been gone for no more than ten minutes and our truck and the Pod trailer already had a fresh half inch of snow. The flakes were the size of quarters and showed no signs of letting up. As we readied the gear I reflected on days spent afield in similar conditions. I remembered a pheasant hunting trip about ten years earlier just outside of Othello with my Dad. We were in a heavy flurry and were hiking towards a patch of cover that was about twenty yards wide and wound through a dirt field. Teal and Comet were hot on scent the entire drive but we had come up empty at the end of the cover. We paused to rest and started to talk to each other discussing how we couldn't believe nothing was in there. The dogs were just sitting there panting looking equally as puzzled. I happened to look down and saw rooster tracks in the snow. I didn't think anything of it for some reason and just walked them out for about ten yards to where they abruptly ended. I called over at Dad and told him to come and check it out. While waiting and still not thinking too much of the situation, I noticed a little hump in the snow. It was clean, no scurrying marks or anything. I figured it was a snow covered rock and kicked it. I had the shock of my life when a monster cock pheasant exploded out from under my foot. I swung my over and under shotgun in pure self defense and shot the bird at about ten feet, blowing out his back. Thankfully the breast was still intact but I had to hike the rest of the day with a bleeding carcass that ended up ruining my pants and shirt. I will never forget the adrenaline rush of that flush or the skill of that pheasant hiding himself so cleverly. Dad said I looked like Tom Knapp doing a trick shot it happened so fast. I later shared a blind with Mr. Knapp and told him that very story. He said there would have been one difference if it had been him. He would have shot that bird twice.

Not too far from where we park there is a little channel deep enough for us to immediately start paddling our Pods. It was still dark and the extra time we had planned allowed us to have a nice leisurely ride. Instead of fighting the slushy conditions the snow on the water was creating in the shallows, we could move out towards the middle and go the long route. I looked like a floating white iceberg. Even the paddle was collecting flakes.

Our primary reason to come to this lake is the Wigeon and Pintail. We have plenty of spots to chase these species, but few can match the flights we have seen descending on this Whatcom County lagoon. Those two ducks out number every other species found in this place easily ten to one. On most good days we will shoot nothing else and ignore the odd Mallard or the occasional Teal. On the south end where the marsh ends and the muds begin we will target Shovelers. Drewry has nicknamed this spot Grinners Hallow. Late in the season we always make it point to try and collect a fully plumed Shoveler, something that is quite hard to do in Washington, but can be accomplished here.

The fact that most Waterfowlers shun the much maligned Shoveler makes it even more special for us in a twisted kind of way, but few will doubt the beauty of a nice prime drake. There are also a few divers on certain weather conditions swinging by for a visit. We have harvested Greater Scaup, Lesser Scaup, Bufflehead, Ruddy ducks, and even a couple of Canvasbacks. For the most part the divers will stick to the middle of the lake and we leave them alone. When we want to lay out for divers we simply have better spots.

I could feel the paddle start to hit the bottom as I came in to the shallows. Jason was coming in behind me and we planned on grassing and hiding the Pods about ten yards from each other. I got out and started walking when paddling was no longer an option and started to do a little strategizing. The ground below the water was surprisingly firm which made it much easier to get around. After marking the area where we were going to set up, I used the Pod as a floating table and walked around the perimeter and dropped my decoys.

We were using our Wigeon and Pintail rig, about six dozen Avery plastics that we set in our familiar pattern. In the past we used to have an all cork and cedar stool but found it was just too much work paddling through the puddle duck areas with that much weight. On this lake we also like a big spread and that simply isn't an option in the traditional manner. When I am sitting in my garage or on the couch thinking of such hunts I always say to myself how disappointed I am in this decision to go back to plastic, but when I am in the field and doing the actual work I am quite content. After all, I bet the old timers if given the choice would have made the same decision.

After dropping the last decoy I turned around to inspect our work. Sure enough, it looked like we had just dropped six dozen snow covered rocks right in the marsh. The snow was piling up as fast as we could knock it off. This summoned forth a blizzard memory of a couple years back. Jason and I were hunting the rocky shores of southern Samish Bay with the same conditions. It was about noon and Jason was limited out. The winds were also howling that day and we couldn't hear each other talk from our rock blinds that were about twenty yards apart. He decided to move to my blind and watch me shoot my last bird.

The day for the both of us was already a huge success. His all drake limit was made up of a few Green Wing Teal, some nicely plumaged Wigeon, and a huge bull Sprig. On the other hand, I was sitting on six perfect drake Wigeon and was waiting for my seventh. I was having Pintail, Teal and Mallard swimming in the decoys the entire time while I was waiting in the blizzard for my rare Samish Wigeon slam. What looked like a pair of Pintails screamed by the spread and showed no interest.

Jason gave a quick call and it turned the smaller darker bird, leaving the drake Sprig to fly off on his own. The bird hooked hard and set right on in without hesitation. I figured it was a hen Pintail until it got close. Then it resembled a young drake Wigeon and that was going to get a free pass too, I wanted nothing but prime drakes. With my gun up I heard Jason yell, "Euro Wigeon!" Panic struck as I pulled the trigger, dropping the bird into the water, not knowing for sure if he was right.

I only knew something just didn't look normal, it just seemed too dark. I was in for a big surprise, he was right. I had shot my first and only European Wigeon to finish out my day. It was a first year drake but I didn't care. It still is one of my favorite mounts in my trophy room. We had to knock the snow off the decoys to pick them up moments after shooting that bird. Now every time I see this I immediately go back in time. Snow on the dekes has never bothered me, it just means I will have to get up every so often for a little maintenance. I'll trade snow for work any day.

First light brought the Pintails. We could hear the soft tones of their familiar whistle. The snow was still coming down at an alarming rate and the first birds of the day were coming in waves high above us and seemingly on mission for somewhere else. In between these flights the silence was surreal. There was no wind, no waves, just the falling flakes in the low lit skies. I closed my eyes and held out my arms. If I could not have felt the cold on my face I would have sworn I wasn't there. The inactivity and the quiet of the moment once again had my mind flooded with the past.

I thought back to when we were teenagers. I think I was either 18 or 19, I can't remember for sure. This makes Jason about 16. At the time we were just started to branch out with hunting on our own. It was a very empowering time for me. Every bird I harvested without the guidance of my Dad seemed like a major victory. It kind of made me feel like I was my own man. I used to race home to show him for his acceptance, and he would always shake my hand and tell me how proud he was. It's what good Dad's do. I think that any guy entering his adult years will know what I mean by these feelings; the independent moments in a young life that you take for granted as you get older and become more jaded.

I had driven Jason up to some farm fields in northern Skagit County where I had received permission to hunt by a local farmer. I had gone a few times on my own without much success, but there were always Mallards in the ditches to jump shoot. This was a huge opportunity for me back then, one that I squandered more than I was successful with. Jason had yet to shoot a nice drake Mallard and had also missed many past attempts. Being young and without resource, boot hunting was just about the coolest thing we could think of doing, and hiking to check those ditches was about as exciting as it got.

When I look back now at our early attempts at Waterfowling I always chuckle how we used to wait for flocks to land so we could sneak up and jump them. It rarely crossed our minds of how much easier placing a few decoys where we knew they were going to be and trying it that route. But as you know how teenage boys are, young, dumb, and full of, well, the energy and the will to hike to no end. I sure wish I had that kind of energy today. Now every time I embark on a hike that is not even one tenth of what I used to do, I start whining for my boat.

The fields were covered in snow from the night before. The ditches had flowing water and were not iced up in the larger areas. This was perfect jump shooting conditions and we set off. The first couple of birds we encountered were flushed wild, there is an art to hunting this way and we hadn't yet mastered this. I used to always say, don't let more water see you that can be in gun range. If the water can see you, so can the ducks. After about an hour of hiking, I managed to back up Jason and connect after he missed on a nice drake Mallard. This only had him more frustrated and as determined as ever.

We crossed a field and came upon a ditch we would later name Greenhead Gully. For some reason, Mallards loved this ditch beyond all others and it was rare there wouldn't be at least a small flock taking up residence. Sometimes there would be hundreds. On this day, there was about twenty, and all of them heard our dragging feet in the crunchy snow and flushed wild. When we got to the ditch I did a quick peek down the way and saw a few birds about a hundred yards down floating in and out of an opening where another ditch intersected with Greenhead Gully, creating a "T". I quickly jumped back and got with Jay. I instructed him to circle wide and showed him where to come in. He could see in my eyes the certainty of this opportunity and I could see him start to tremble. I tried to calm him down and told him to go as slow as he could. Quiet was the factor.

I remember watching him slowly close the gap to that ditch as he hiked. With every step he got more in gun range. Surprisingly, he managed to go all the way to the edge. I can only imagine how those Mallards felt looking up at Jason only feet away. During his walk it had started snowing and for sure this had confused those birds who most surely had heard him coming. I watched as he brought up his gun and the flock of over a hundred Mallards exploded from the snowy ground. His first shot sent a bird straight down. His second came after a great pause as he excitedly tried to pump his old Remington 870 Wingmaster. By that time the birds were well out of gun range and nothing fell. I ran as fast as I could to get there, only to find him with a very sullen look on his face.

"I missed! How could I miss! I will never get a chance like this again!"

I was puzzled at his ranting. He all but fell over in the snow in disgust.

"Missed? What? Is that a hen you dropped on your first shot?" I asked.

"I never hit anything!"

That is when I realized he was so excited and caught up in the moment he had no idea there was a dead bird floating in the water. At first the only rational thought I had watching him being so upset was that he had dropped a hen and that his trophy first drake was long gone. I crossed my fingers as I ran to the ditch to fetch the bird he didn't know existed. Sure enough, there was a big bull Mallard floating lifeless. I crawled down, grabbed the bird, and tossed it up to him.

He let out the largest yell of excitement I have ever heard, I bet the farmer was wondering just what the heck we were doing out there. We sat there in the snow for over an hour admiring our two drake Mallards we had in hand. It was this bird that we later took to get mounted. This is where I fell in love with the art of taxidermy. I still remember vividly walking through his showroom thinking to myself that I had to do this, there was just no option. Five years later I had my taxidermy license.

Two drake Pintails came swooping down, and were gone as fast as they appeared. The light was still low and everything remained a dark solemn gray. Jason had just returned from cleaning up the decoys as best he could and was not ready for the shot. The snow had me hypnotized; I needed to snap out of it and focus.

There are a few ways to positively identify a nice bull Sprig in these conditions and it was going to take all of that experience this morning. The first and the obvious is the size difference when they come in as pairs. The hen is always shorter and smaller with a somewhat compact tail. The drake will appear longer and sleeker, with the tail end seemingly extended no matter how big his sprig may be. Unfortunately, they don't always come in as pairs. The next thing I look for is his neck. In low light the neck of a nice drake will appear missing. It will look as if the head is not connected to the body. This of course is his white markings on the neck giving the illusion of space. The last option is actually watching for tails. We decoy Pintails at close ranges and after some experience it is not difficult to see his sprig silhouette in the dark. We don't just want to shoot a Pintail, but we go after the big boys. With a one bird limit in an area where there are many, many birds, you have to take every precaution. It is that attention to detail that allows you to take the best birds and make your bag consistently more productive.

"John, right there, to your right!"

"Where?" As soon as I had asked that, he took a shot and dropped a nice Pintail right into the middle of the spread.

"Right there!" We both laughed and I walked out and got his bird. It was my turn to do a little snow maintenance on the dekes.

When I got back into my Pod the Pintails were every where. There were groups of five, ten, twenty, circling and landing all around us. I froze and enjoyed the moment. A hen swam about five feet from the end of my small boat totally oblivious of us. I was focused on that one special bird in all the flocks but was having a hard time feeling good about taking any kind of shot. I leaned up and spooked the birds swimming in the decoys, trying to flush them away. Confused, they simply started circling again and landed, only this time outside the decoys. The flights seemed to calm down a bit as a group of four locked. They banked a little left and that is when I saw him. His sprig stuck out like a red dress in a black and white photo. It seemed so ridiculously large I would have sworn there was an Oldsquaw mixed up with the wrong crowd. At the split second I saw him I could hear Jason yelling "Shoot that one! Shoot that one!"

I sat up and pulled the trigger. The old boy broke away from the rest and headed directly behind me. I could see him lumbering away as I took my second shot trying to swing around while sitting in my Pod. When that missed I had to completely twist around to the other side and pull up again. My third shot finally sent him tumbling into the marsh bushes, I could hear him crash all the way down to the ground. It sounded as if he were fifty pounds forced out of the sky.

When I reached him I couldn't believe his size. I put him against the drake Jason had shot moments earlier and it looked like it was easily twice as big. The tail was long, one of the longest I had ever seen. It wasn't just the length that had me so excited, it was the girth. I couldn't believe the thickness of this sprig. We shoot and hold a lot of Pintails during our Waterfowl seasons, and I have yet to see one this big.

We sat there for another half hour watching Pintail after Pintail splash and swim around. The occasional Mallard and a few flocks of Wigeon set in but we were so elated with our Pintails and the wildness of the blizzard that we decided to pack it in early. The long drive home almost matched the drama of the morning hunt. People just aren't ready when snow hits in Washington and for that you have to be a little patient on our highways.

I ended up mailing out my trophy Pintail to a taxidermist friend named Blake Wilson of Wings Over Water Studios in Alabama. He is one of the finest flight taxidermists I know and I wanted this bird to have the justice it deserves. I enjoy having other taxidermists work on my birds and have only recently decided I want to start collecting others work just like I do with decoys. I am sure when Blake put the Pintail into his freezer he chuckled. One part of taxidermy all of us have to deal with is hearing folks say "this is the largest Mallard I have ever seen!" Everyone thinks their trophy is a monster and unique, and I, like many others, just smile and tell them how right they are as I put yet another normal mature drake into my freezer. When I was on the phone with Blake I could sense he was feeling the same way and smiled, but I didn't change my course of conversation. To me, it was the biggest sprig I had ever seen, my monster.

Hunting in the snow is probably the most rewarding way I can think of to spend the day in the field. It evokes in me a passion like no other. When I find myself looking skyward at the gray clouds, watching the flakes come towards my face, I drift into another realm. Call me old fashioned, even a sap, but is moments like that where I really feel alive.

Chapter 15

Canvasback Opener

If you ever find yourself in a blind with me I will guarantee you one thing. I will ask you the same question I have asked of everyone that came before you. It goes like this; if there could only be one bird out of all winged creatures on the planet left to hunt and you got to choose to hunt just this one bird, what would it be? I don't think I have ever had the same answer twice with the exception of the Mallard and with that answer I usually respond with a heartfelt "I'm so sorry for you." One notable reply came from longtime friend Jeffery Brown, who I think mentioned some Crane species from Africa. I would bet that if I asked him that question three times a year for ten years I would have a different response every time. In fact, I think I have.

I can recall hunting with our state DU Treasurer, Troy Wiley and he chose the Canada goose which I thought was kind of boring, especially since he knocks the crud out of them every year. I guess he is living his dream. Another that comes to mind was Brad Otto, an employee of the WDFW and a good friend through the WWA, who said the Wood Duck. I could handle Wood Ducks on an every hunt basis. I don't think I would be satisfied if that was all though, they are almost a little too flashy and a bit on the common side of things in most states. A year later I remember asking him again and this time he said Mallard. I haven't had the desire to hunt with him since . . . I'm just kidding Brad.

Eventually the question always gets turned back around and I have to answer. Without hesitation I will tell you will full conviction, the Canvasback. From the first time I saw one in the wild to the last drake to visit my spread, they have inspired a passion in me like none other. The regal way they hold their head high with such a thick chestnut neck demands that they be called the King of Ducks. From a history perspective they hold a high reverence in past writings and claim more tradition in North America than all the rest. Even the taste of their flesh is held in high regard, they were the highest priced breast filet in the old market gunning days at the turn of the twentieth century. Just the mention of Canvasbacks has me day dreaming of a time gone by of old wood decoys, paper shells and a classic side by side shotgun.

Here in Washington there is a long history of Canvasbacks being closed for the season for one reason or another. They were recently re-opened once again in 2003 after a couple of years being restricted. Canvasbacks are a sensitive breeder and the populations can fluctuate from year to year. They demand good sound management and personally I really enjoy the one bird a day limit they currently deploy. I treat every outing chasing Cans as a trophy hunt and try to only shoot the best Silverback drake I can find. Washington currently follows the Pacific Flyway split season giving us two openers. For the first week of the season they are open, then close and don't open back up until December. Jason and I usually ignore them that first week and concentrate on the late season when their plumage will be in prime shape. We treat the December opener as the second kick off to the season and go all out much like the first opening weekend. When hunting Cans in Western Washington, we have a spot that is only an hour away and we get a group together that stays at a local hotel for the night before. We fill the evening with wild meat barbeques and the annual Canvasback Open, a poker tournament that is my probably my favorite of the year. Mostly because the winner gets first shot the next morning.

Canvasbacks are dispersed throughout the entire state in Washington with the bulk of the population migrating through the Columbia River from the Canadian border down to the mouth out of Ilwaco. Most eastern Washington Rivers will hold at least small groups with the most notable the Snake River, and we have hunted in most of those areas. On the west side most Cans are found on lakes and some back sloughs. I know when certain fields flood in the Snohomish River Valley some ardent Can hunters will be out in force as small groups will congregate to feed. There are a few flocks on the salts of the Sound, but I would call those more incidental little groups than anything else. I would hardly say we have the numbers or the traditions of say the Chesapeake Bay or the famed Pool 9 on the Mississippi river but as a state we can definitely hold our own. In respect to Pool 9 we named our best lake in its honor. We took out the 9 that follows Pool and replaced it with the represented amount of Cans taken by us and our guests while hunting this spot. After a few years the name reached Pool 99 and at that point the name was retired. We settle on the simple name of the "Can Hole" currently. Not really imaginative but it gets the job done when trying to identify the unnamed lake when discussing the hunt in our circle of friends.

I met Jason at his house in the afternoon the day before the opener. We have been anticipating this all season long and now it was upon us. I was a little early and we were in no rush so we decided to pull out the decoys and make sure one last time they were looking their best. In all honesty, I will take any excuse to look at the many works of art we have in this collection. Of all the rigs we will set in the water our Can stool is by far the rig I enjoy the most. In the off season they all have a special shelf in my trophy room but not now. They are rigged up and ready to go. I am trying to collect as many handmade Silverback cork and wood decoys from across the country and beyond from fellow Can hunters. If you hunt Cans and carve, I bet I will be bugging you soon. Jason and I have only been collecting for a couple of years but we are already fortunate to have the carvers of the likes of Jeff Coats, Tom Matus, Mike Prawdzik, Dave Drewry, Brad Forgey, Gary March, Don Spidell, Chris Engelhardt, Jason Barnett, Cory Herendeen, Bob Hayden, Josh Ward, Tom Newell, Ed Lindsay, and Ben Welton represented on the water. Mixed in are several from Jason he has carved throughout the years. My personal favorite is my Jason Otto number one decoy. The first bird he ever carved, a nice little cork Can. Every time I pull it out of the slotted bag he gives me a sneer and a look of "retire that already". "No way" I always say, this hunt is all about tradition, and does it get any better than that?

We gathered up our gear and headed out. On the way to the hotel I called up Drewry to make one last check to see if he was in or not. The dates for this opener come out after he books his clients and sure enough he was all locked up. I knew he didn't like to miss this hunt but I wasn't too worried, we had two months of the season left and it wouldn't be to hard to get him out for Cans. Our "Can Hole" is pretty consistent until it freezes over, and that usually doesn't happen until mid to late January. Jason called the cousins Engelhardt and Cummings who were already on their way. Chris had a nice spread as well made up mostly of his own creations. Rounding out the party was Ben Welton. Ben hadn't been on a Can hunt in years and we insisted he joined us. It didn't take much arm twisting and we were looking forward to getting him out in the field after some health problems had him on hiatus for a couple of weeks.

The night breezed on by and after a couple of rousing games of Texas-Hold-Um with the group I was wore out. I went to bed a little earlier than usual only to stare at the darkened ceiling. The anxiety I get before hunting such a majestic bird is at times is too much to bear. All the memories of past hunts just flood my mind to a point I relive almost every detail. It was one of those nights when you remember looking over at the alarm clock and see midnight, one, two, three, and basically try to beg yourself to get to sleep. I awoke from my mini naps about ten minutes before the alarm was to go off. Instead of lying there waiting I just got out of bed and started getting ready.

"John, are you O.K.?" asked a startled Jason. He knows how much I am not a morning person. "Is it time to get up?"

"Yeah, couldn't sleep. Sorry if I woke you too soon."

"Are you kidding me, I have been sitting here for over an hour. Let's do this." He popped right out of bed and joined me.

In moments we were heading to the parking lot ready to go. Much to our surprise, Chris and Kasey were already at their truck. I looked down at my watch to see it was exactly a half an hour earlier than the time we had given to meet each other. We all laughed and headed out. Upon our arrival there was Ben sitting in the gravel driveway waiting for us. This didn't surprise me, I figured if we were an hour early he still would have beat us.

Our "Can Hole" is basically a large lake that looks like it is cut out of a mountain side with the western shore surrounded by trees. If you were to look at it from an aerial map you would see that it is in close proximity to the salt, so close it only takes moments of flight to get there. The Canvasbacks will roost on the salt and spend the day feeding on the lake. When we give them any kind of pressure they retreat to the salt only to return about twenty minutes later. On a good year this lake winters about 400 Cans which is a rather large congregation for the Pacific Flyway. Especially large when you consider we have the place to ourselves unlike most of the river hunting on the east side of the state that can get rather competitive. The access to this body of water is extremely limited. The use of small man carried boats is the only way to get to where the birds are. This also unfortunately limits our guests to those with such boats. Ben was in his second year with his Aqua-Pod, the same boat we have been using for years. Chris had to share a ride with Kasey who owns a Fatboy DP from Momarsh. This thirteen footer requires a little more help getting it to and from the water but is quite roomy and held the two "Fatboys" rather well.

Getting the gear and the boats to the water requires a little hike down a steep embankment that is a little treacherous. After we all assisted each other to the shore line we got together and made a plan. Jason and I were going to hunt the west side about fifty yards apart with our own little spread and Ben was going to set up on the north end in the tall tulle reeds. The cousins took the southeast portion of the lake, in a little cove where the stream that feeds the body of water lies. A week before I had driven by and did a little bit of scouting and found birds in just about every nook and cranny. I figured any spot was as good as any at this point.

    I slid my little skiff into the water and in I hopped. There wasn't a cloud in the sky and the reflection of the moon off the glass like conditions was very bright. I slowly dipped my paddle into the water trying not to disturb the calm as much as possible. I looked over at my brother who just so happened to be watching me at the same time. He gave me a quick head nod of satisfaction. We were Canvasback hunting. I decided to take lead and headed us out into the open water to get to the other side.

    About half way there I broke off and went to my little corner. Even in the dark you could see where the Cans were diving and digging up the little potato bud seeds in the aquatic plants leaving the leafy vines floating on the surface. It becomes so thick in spots it is hard to paddle through. My whole area was about four feet deep, a constant depth all the way to the shore. Once at the shore the land stood about two feet off the water making it a perfect place to snug up the Pod and hide in the jagged little coves. I placed the three dozen corkers in a wind swept sort of motion and began to place the vegetation on the outer part of my boat for concealment. I made sure the farthest decoy was no more than thirty yards away to keep all my shots in close gunning range.

    I was ready to go. I looked down at my watch to see that I still had forty five minutes left until opening gun. Forty five minutes is a long time, way too long. I could see Ben's headlamp off to my left. It was going all over the place and he was obviously still setting up. The marsh noises were surprisingly quiet and tranquil. I decided I would reach down into my blind bag and pull out a cigar. It was a little early to be doing this but I couldn't take the wait, I had to do something. The long cool draws seemed to calm my nerves. I called over to Jason on the two-way to see how he was doing.

    "Hey Jay, you out there?"

    "Yeah, I got you," he whispered back, "you won't believe this but I already have a pair swimming in the decoys!"

    "Oh man, how cool. That's got to be a good sign. What time you got?"

    He chuckled over the radio, "I have a half hour to go too. Why the heck did we get here so early?"

    A little while later I noticed four birds of my own swimming around. I had no idea where they came from and could barely tell what they were. Before I could positively identify them they were gone. After that I could hear wings cutting through the air all around me. The beats were fast and deliberate, I knew what those were. In an instant I had twenty birds land ten yards outside my rig. I once again looked down at my watch; I now only had five minutes to go.

"Jay, you there?"

"Can't talk, birds everywhere!"

I set the radio down and watched my visitors. All of a sudden another large flock dropped in on the others. Then more came. Before I knew it I had about a hundred Cans dancing and playing not more than twenty yards from where I sat. I could now see the males from females and could even differentiate the Silverbacks, the prime drakes. I was astonished at what I saw. I knew I had to be patient, with a one bird limit there was no way I could cleanly shoot at any drake if they were to flush. I was wondering what the rest of the crew were seeing. Another glance at my watch, it was now shooting time.

For about ten minutes I just sat there, trying to be as still as I could. A few were diving and feeding already while most were content to just swim in small circles around each other. There were Mallards and Wigeon hovering above in massive circles looking for a place to land. A few would trickle down and join the Canvasbacks, but most headed out to the open water. I followed one drake Mallard that I easily could have taken. Not now, not today. I just watched him as he drifted to the middle of the lake. Before he landed I got crossed up with another bird that was headed directly to my location. As it got closer and I could tell it was a Can. The bird dipped down to a couple of feet off the water as it approached the large flock. When it hit the edge of the spread, it lifted up like it wanted to land square in the middle, right over the backs of his brethren. It was a perfect Silverback and he was all alone, a perfect shot. I pulled up and dropped him at about ten yards. He fell into the chaos that erupted all around. It was so busy and loud, I didn't see my Can hit the water. Then I heard another shot, it was Jason. It was a single shot and I thought that had to be good.

I quickly paddled over and picked up my bird. In my excitement I just threw him on my blind bag and sped over to meet up with Jason as quick as I could. When I got around the bend I saw he was heading my way. We met in the middle and headed to shore. Once there I pulled out my Canvasback by the feet and gave him a good shake to get all the water off. He was a real beauty. The nape of his neck had the fullest burnt orange feathers all the way down to his striking black chest. The body was large and chunky. His wings had the whitish hues on the outside feathers, one of the last markings of an old bird. Everything about him shouted bull. Jason's matched mine equally, two prime specimens.

Normally we would leave as soon as this moment was over. We don't put any unnecessary pressure on this spot and leave all other species alone. I called Chris and Kasey on their radio to see how things were going. They hadn't seen a diver yet and were getting tired of passing on Mallard after Mallard. We instructed them move to my spot and I joined Jason to kick back over his rig while we waited them out. A little while later we broke our own rule when a young drake Redhead set in the rig. Jason made quick work on the harvest. On the east side Redheads are quite plentiful where you find Cans and we target them often but on our side seeing a Redhead is a rare occurrence. The two drakes look good together and it was a nice little bonus.

It took about twenty minutes before we heard a volley of shots fired from where I had been. A trio came in and the cousins doubled on their drakes. We picked up and joined them while waiting for Ben. I paddled over to check on him to find he was knee deep in hens and juveniles. I hung out and talked Cans with him for a while and then headed out. On my way back I heard a single shot. I paddled around to see another Silverback flopping in the water. The day was a complete success.

We quickly picked up all the spreads. The commotion we created forced the Canvasbacks to the middle of the lake out into the open water. When all was done and we were driving away I looked back to see them feeding where we had set up, as if the morning hunt had never happened. At breakfast we spent more time reliving the morning hunt than it actually took to happen. That's how it goes with Canvasbacks.

The next morning Jason and I hosted Waterfowl biologist Brad Bortner of the U.S. Fish and Wildlife at the very same slice of heaven and at the very shore edge of the day before. That little amount of pressure we had put on the Cans had them acting completely different. This time it took us until 11:00 in the morning to get our three birds and the once incoming large flocks were now broken down into small groups of three to five. The highlight of that day was watching Brad take his Canvasback with his father's old Parker side by side 12 gauge over an old unidentified turn of the century cedar block that he had sitting in his office for years. I felt like it was a hundred years earlier as I watched him set the bird, decoy and gun on an old stump to take a picture.

After taking eight Canvasbacks in two days we decided to rest the lake for a couple of weeks to keep the birds in town. This was good news to Captain Dave. We didn't return until he was able to go.

There is something about hunting Canvasbacks. It's magical, mystical, and most rewarding in so many traditional ways. I can honestly say without hesitation if there was only one bird left to hunt I know what I would choose.

Chapter 16

Lost at Sea

Some rewards of Waterfowling are earned through experience, hard work, and sheer grit. Others, well, can sort of fall into your lap. There is a lot of truth to the old adage better lucky than smart. On this particular hunt, I would find out just how lucky a guy can be.

We have a goal of finding a beach spot for every type of waterfowl we hunt. This goal really met our match when it came to the Long Tail Duck, or Oldsquaw. A lot of our hunts for the little sea sprig found us miles out in the open salt water in some of the deepest water you could set a long line. Harvesting a bird that is so well known for open water on the shore kind of became an obsession. Year after years of scouting had produced nothing of merit, and we were about to give up. The closest we came was a puddle duck hunt years earlier that was actually somewhat near some noted Squaw haunts.

A SEASON OF WING-SHOOTING

It was the strangest thing; a lone hen swam into our decoys from the open water and died. She just plopped her head down as soon as she reached the decoys and was finished without us firing a shell. Upon retrieval we noticed it had been a cripple, and judging by her body weight she had been like that for some time. Although it was neat to see an Oldsquaw in our bag that day in our marsh blind, we knew that didn't count. This was someone else's bird, and for sure would have had nothing to do with the rig if she was healthy.

Our most often used waters for Longtail are on the north end of a bay that is little used or even recognized stretch of open water that most Waterfowlers wouldn't think held anything of significance. These northern spots are unique for us in the fact we are only about a hundreds yards from the shore at times if the flights allow. There is a small under water channel the birds like to work and feed that twists from the open bay to near the shore, and we took full advantage. The beach seemed so close, but every attempt we made turned into a bird watching event, watching them fly up and down that channel and laughing as they would never even venture close. We decided it was time to better scout the north east end, an area we had always shied away from, and about another ten miles away. The water is unprotected by land, and quite remote. There is a series of small islands which are neat, but getting there is always difficult and usually not worth the effort. We had an afternoon to kill and calm seas. Scouting that area seemed like the thing to do so we set out.

When we arrived we found a few small pockets of Squaw, nothing that was too exciting. Jason also made the observation that there wasn't much else in the way of other duck species. All this was adding up to just a nice boat ride. About to give up, we saw it. On the north tip of one of the islands was a point with about fifty birds. They couldn't have been more than fifty feet off shore. I kicked the motor down and slowly shuffled up. A couple of drakes that had been underwater arose in flight and began to fly around the point to get away. We had found our spot, or at least we hoped we did. These birds were obviously flying close to that point when trading waters and the beach was a perfect place to set up a blind. We quickly decided to be there first thing in the morning and give it a go. The weather was to be a concern, any type of wind and there was simply no way to get to this remote area. That night when looking at the atlas we realized we were basically hunting the mouth of the Strait of Juan de Fuca. It doesn't get more open than that.

The morning couldn't have been more perfect. Bone chilling cold and zero wind. The bay was eerily calm looking like glass, and quite lit up by the full moon. We arrived early and set up. I tried to drop the lines from the beach only to find out the tide was a bit fuller than the prior day and finished the job from the boat. All the while Jason worked on the blind. There were plenty of natural materials on this island. The shore had several large rocks and driftwood was littered everywhere at the high tide mark. This made his job easy. The whole hunt was coming together nicely, almost too easy for such a new spot. We were ready to go a good half hour before opening gun. We killed the time with a nice cigar and talked of all the Oldsquaw hunts we have had in our past. They are such a fun and challenging bird to hunt.

The sunrise was especially majestic. Glowing oranges and reds seared through the morning sky. I kept thinking of how lucky we were here to enjoy this. I wondered how many people had actually even been to this place. We weren't the first for sure, but there can't have been many. It seems untouched, very wild. So wild in fact, that in all directions not a trace of civilization can be seen. I like it. I tried to imagine we had gone back in time and were experiencing a moment the first settlers experienced. Maybe they sat on this very beach trying to harvest their dinner for the evening.

"John, do you see anything?" Jason quickly brought me out of my trance. His rhetorical question was right; there wasn't a bird in sight. The usual tell tale signs of hunting Oldsquaw were hearing them as they assembled into the area, and all I could hear were the small waves lapping into the sand.

"Wow, someone forget to tell the Jack-ow-lees to cooperate!"

I stood up and took a look around, there was nothing. Not a sound, not even a sea gull. Where had these birds gone in just one day? Who can tell, I thought. Those that hunt Oldsquaw know how finicky and unpredictable they can be. Today was just not in the cards. I was alright with that. This spot was amazing and I wasn't in any hurry to leave.

"Hey, do you see that bird down the beach?" Jason pointed. I could see it, feeding away and oblivious to us being there. It was probably a hundred and fifty yards out, maybe ten yards off shore. He had either swam in or snuck up from behind us. The light was a bit bright off the water and I couldn't make a good ID, but I assumed it to be a nice drake as big as it was.

"Go see if you can sneak up on it Jay," I said, "I bet you won't get close."

"Too early for a desperation jump shoot, it's all yours."

I decided I agreed with him. We are not much for jumping birds out side the rig, and a part of me was still thinking that nice little flock of Squaw would be coming around the bend at any second. Besides, the odds of successfully sneaking up on a feeding Squaw were slim to none. Been there, tried that, only to walk back empty handed.

Another ten minutes went by and the only action we had was that lone feeder. A guy can only watch the sunrise for so long, a walk would be nice anyhow. "Alright, I'll give it a go." A slight chuckle from Jay and I was off.

I timed his dives and moved down the beach while he was down. When he would pop up, I froze. I still couldn't get a good look with all the sun glare but had seen enough to know something wasn't quite right. How embarrassing it would be if I ended my stalk and found a loon or some other type of sea bird. Jason would never let me live it down.

As I got to about fifty yards, I definitely knew something wasn't right. I was seeing way too much black for a Squaw, and the bird just looked too big. A Scoter I thought? No, too much light colors near the breast and head. The sun was killing me. He dove once again. This time I broke into a run to meet him on the beach. I got to the edge and up he came, this time he was in mid-flight as he broke from the water, he must have felt me coming. At this point, I knew exactly what it was. A drake King Eider!

I shot on pure instinct. I hit him as he was lifting in air after a long run. He immediately dove. My heart dove with him. He popped up quickly, probably as shocked as I was. My second shot was a swat shot, the spread went all around him. He dove again. He was about thirty yards off shore now and I knew I needed help. He would be out of range quick and there wasn't much time.

"Jason!" I screamed as loud as I could, "Get the boat!"

I could see there wasn't much intensity in his actions. After all, nothing worse than having to go through all the work of uncloaking the boat, drag it back in the water, and go chase what he obviously thought was a crippled Squaw that I had just jump shot. Chasing crippled Squaw is just no fun.

"Jay, it is a King!" I think I said it in sheer terror, trying to get him to put a hitch in the giddy up.

"No way," he yelled back rather inquisitively. "What?"

My arms couldn't wave any harder. He popped up again. This time about fifty yards out. I knew I had hit him pretty good judging by the feathers left on the calm water after the first shot, but this is a sea duck. One shot means nothing. I touched one off, only to see the pattern vaguely surround him. Where is a full choke when you need one? He dove again.

Jason quickly had the boat in route now, and met me at the shore. I jumped in and he headed towards the open water.

"Jay, I swear, I just shot a King Eider!" I was beginning to hyperventilate a bit and was shaking all over. He could tell there was no way I was kidding. His face still showed extreme doubt, but he knew my urgency was at full tilt. Urgency turned to panic, he was no where to be seen. Seconds seemed like hours. Was I totally wrong? Was my mind playing tricks on me? It wasn't everyday you see a King Eider; I certainly began to doubt myself. Would Jason ever believe me?

"Over there! Holy wow! There it is, shoot it!" Jason just about fell out of the boat as the panic had now spread to him. I had to turn around, find the bird which was now about 40 yards away, and touched another shot off. Again, he dove.

"Quarter over this way, to the right!" I was trying to use every bit of skill I had ever learned chasing crippled sea ducks. Guessing their path, and guessing correctly, was the best chance of finishing him off.

"Right there!" Of course I had guessed wrong and we headed in another direction. This game of cat and mouse lasted long enough for me to take another four shots on the boat. The final shot sent feathers everywhere. As a taxidermist, I feared the worse. As a hunter, I felt the exhilaration that this bird was done, he was now floating on the water. I reached down and grabbed him by his feet, shaking off all the water and blood. I laid him down on the bench seat of the boat, and just tried to compose myself. He was absolutely gorgeous. A bit shot up, but perfect none the less. He had a rich blue head, dark black back, the white pinkish chest, fully mature. I made eye contact with Jason; we were both in utter disbelief. We didn't say a word that could be repeated here, and we just smoked another cigar to calm ourselves down.

When we got back to the beach, I tried to call Captain Dave. I tried to call Dad. I tried to call everyone. We were far from cell service and we made the decision that we must leave. I think Jason wanted to stay for a bit in case another King just happened to wonder by, and for sure we took the long way back, looking all over. When I finally got a hold of Dave I made his wife Tiffany roust him out of the shower. This was simply too important to wait, even a mere minute was longer than I could stand. I put a lot of time on my phone that day.

To decompress, we drove to a little beach and threw out a couple of decoys. All I wanted to do was stare at my King, and this was a great way to do it. We ended up shooting a limit that afternoon of Mallards, Greater Scaup, and a few Buffleheads. The fact we didn't even see one Squaw all day was quite alright by me. I was so excited when I got home I immediately mounted the bird. It was shot in the morning and on my mantle in my trophy room that very night where it still stands today. Knowing this bird came from the Arctic, most likely hitching a ride with an unsuspecting Long Tail or a wayward Surf Scoter, and coming all the way down to Washington reminded me of that old saying once again. "It is better to be lucky than smart". And I am living proof of that. What is that other old cliché'? Even a blind squirrel finds a nut now and then? I sure love my nut!

About every other year in Washington there are sightings of wayward King Eiders on our shores. Three years ago a nice drake was spotted a couple of days in a row in the south west Washington bay of Gray's Harbor by a couple of bird watchers who posted their find on the internet. Last year a young drake, still adorning its drab brown juvenile plumage, was sighted north in the waters west of the border town of Blaine just off shore. A picture of this bird made the local paper. At the same time we were hearing of another lone fully plumaged drake being photographed by biologists studying Surf Scoters off Vancouver Island up in Canada. While sightings are really rare, a harvest is almost a one in a million chance that has not yet fully sunk in for me, and most likely never will. If there is another such harvest in Washington State, I have not heard of it. At the same time, I am sure it is bound to happen again as Sea Ducking continues to grow in popularity spreading more guns throughout the bays. Captain Dave has often joked with me that maybe I shot the entire state's population. I certainly hope that isn't the case!

Jason hasn't turned down a chance to "walk the beach" since.

Chapter 17

The Christmas Goose

  I know it's not really kosher to mix the term karma in with a holiday like Christmas Eve. But I will be honest; we have felt positive cosmic forces working for us on this particular day for years. For some reason this day always holds a little bit of luck and good fortune for us Otto boys. I say luck because somewhere, somehow, we have always squeezed in a hunt that turns out to be one of the best of the year on a day that should be all but impossible to get out on.
  Karma may be a factor. Perhaps our great fortune is a reward for doing good things for others. Thinking over the last year I believe Jason and I have that covered. But I just can't imagine God would want to reward two brothers, who should probably be helping their wives with the last minute details of Christmas, with a great shoot on Christmas Eve day. Maybe I am wrong about that. Either way, all I know is I wouldn't miss this hunt for anything.
  To even get out on a day like this you must first confront the many obstacles that will surely present themselves. The first situation you have to overcome is your family. Not only do you have to convince them this is a good idea for you to go, if they agree, will have to contend with the fact they will want you to be home early.
  It is also a given that you had better not display any sign being tired later on that night. Revealing that you are tired because you were slogging through the mud and the gunk of your favorite swamp while your wife provided all

the fixings and trimmings for an unforgettable family gathering can only end badly. Trust me on this one.

Another obstacle is that I always seem to have to work that morning. That goes for Jason too. I can never catch a break no matter how hard I try and schedule myself the day off. Both of us manage people for a living, and they all have the same goal as we do on that day, get home. This always leaves a very small window of opportunity. So why do we even bother?

Ok, let's look at this positively. There are a couple of things in our favor as a hunter on this holiday. Most sane husbands wouldn't think to grab their shotgun and attempt to pull off what we do, not when there are so many other things going on. Right there we are money ahead. I don't think I have ever seen another hunter out in the field in the many years we have been doing this. People that know us would say that we "hunt where people don't go" and that it makes our point invalid. That may be slightly true, but we have driven by some of the more popular public hunting lands on the way to our spots and have verified this. There is nobody there.

We have seen first hand that there is not anyone as dumb as us. Well, how about as driven . . . you know what I mean. Still, I keep hoping that we can find someone else with our passion, if for no other reason I can go home and tell my wife that we are not alone.

Another thought, and I know this may sound a bit on the selfish side, is that I consider this a nice little Christmas present to myself. After all, I deserve this day, don't I? It's not like Toni is going to let me go Christmas morning, so I should be able to, right? Alright, maybe I better not go down this path. It has been pointed out to me that when you hunt as much as I do the word "deserve" should not be used.

Now I should go into the history a bit. In order to go through so much hassle on such a big holiday, there has to be a great reason, and there is. Back when Jason and I were teenagers, we went out in the middle of the day for what we thought would be a stolen a moment of solitude. It looked like a terrible day to go hunting. The sun was out, it felt like 60 degrees, and the tide was so low that you could see hundreds of yards of mud at Samish Bay.

There was absolutely no way a bird should have been flying. We hiked out to the middle of the dike with six decoys and placed them in a little patch of sheet water about thirty yards out. When we got there I didn't see a bird in the sky. For the first half hour it went about as expected, we had nothing and saw the same. Then one duck came, then two. Groups started to appear out of nowhere, and then downright huge flocks and all of them wanted in this little mud puddle.

Before we knew what had happened, there were eight perfect drake Wigeon lined up on the dike. This was back when the Pacific Flyway limits were four a day. We just couldn't believe our luck. It was at that moment we swore we would hunt Christmas Eve together for the rest of our lives, no matter what. At the time we were not sure what our futures held or if we would even be living next to each other as the years were to roll on. We made a vow in blood and have stuck to that ever since. Well, maybe not in blood, but we did do a "pinky swear". That's close enough.

The very next year we had the same results. It was still a four bird limit and we went to the exact same spot. This time we had a bit of weather on our side, it was cold, windy and rainy. Again we shot eight perfect drake Wigeon. The year after that, we both shot our first Canvasbacks out of a slough with a mere ten minutes before shooting hours were over. This gave us our limits in less than an hour after a very late start. We just could not seem to fail.

One season Jason and I invited a longtime friend and fellow taxidermist Jeffery Brown to join us. At the time he had never shot an Oldsquaw and it was high on his want list. The weather prevented taking him to our "A" spot and we had to settle on a safe little Scoter hunt miles from any where near I had ever seen a Long-tail. Sure enough, the last two birds to decoy were two of the finest Squaws on the water and we both got trophies. It seems our karma rubs off on anyone we take as well. Year after year the success rate on this holiday is staggering, and mostly just unexplainable. It doesn't matter if we have all morning or just a quick hour, we now expect something cool to happen.

Fast forward to the present and once again it is the day before Christmas Eve, and we are plotting and planning. This year we are fortunate to almost have all day. There is no work and no problems. We had been saving a little beach on a remote section of Possession Bay that was holding a huge flock of Common Goldeneyes. All our Common harvest this season had been primarily incidentals and I was itching to specifically target them. Jason had just carved a few new hollowed out cedar GE dekes and this was the perfect time to get them wet. I stopped over at his house to check them out and after hanging out for a while we decided to call Drewry to see if he could join us. After a couple of attempts I finally got him on the phone.

"Hey Captain, how are you doing? Are you ready for Christmas?" I figured I better get a feeling of where he was mentally before I try and drag him away for the day. You just never know where people are at in the head around the holidays, I didn't want to add to any stress.

"You know what? I am doing great. All my shopping is done, the boys shopping is done. I have no clients for a couple of days, life is good. How about you?" It was good to hear him so relaxed. I could tell he was going to be an easy sell.

"I am in the same boat, all done. I hung out with Kaden and Abi last night and we got everything we need for Toni. They just love shopping for

Mom. Now all I got to do is have a good hunt tomorrow and Christmas will be all good!" I was still easing into asking.

"Oh yeah, I forgot you guys have your big "holiday" hunt every year. You guys are crazy. I don't know how you pull that one off."

Uh-oh, I thought. No time to hold punches now. "That's why I am calling. Jay and I want you to come this year. It won't be the same without you and we got some Goldeneyes stacked. Let's go!"

There was a bit of a pause on the phone. I could tell he was mulling over his chances. This one is tricky. I know this well. Even asking could send most wives over the edge. You have to do it carefully. One strategy is the old "I was only kidding dear", but this only works if you jump on it quickly at the first sight of a sneer right after asking. Another is to play it coy, see if she suggests it to you. Who am I kidding; I don't know of any wives that would "suggest" you leave her on this holiday.

"Hmmm... oh man that sounds good. I need a good shoot. Just a second." I could hear him put the phone down to his side and call out to Tiffany. This took guts to do the abrupt yell. I quickly thought of how I was now dead meat if she was mad, it would be my fault for the suggestion. "Hey, I will see you guys in the morning, no problem!"

"Serious? That's sweet! Just get there as soon as you can, we will keep the blind warm. Are you sure there aren't any problems?" I just had to ask. The last thing I want is a friend's wife mad at me. I love Tiffany and wouldn't want her upset. Same thing goes for Jay's wife Tanya; I would rather have Jason and Dave mad at me rather than those two. They are much prettier.

"Actually she thought it was a good idea as long as I am home early enough. She didn't think twice. Do you mind if I bring Spence? I would love to spend the day with him too." The nonchalant tone in his voice said it all. It pays to marry well was all I could think. Maybe I am over reacting to this day? Maybe I should ask my wife for a quick Christmas morning hunt and let the kids sleep in a bit? Maybe, well maybe I should thank my lucky stars I married well too and not push my luck.

"We would love to have Spence. See you in the morning..."

The location of this hunt will cause Dave to miss the first light shoot and most likely the first half hour or so due to his ferry ride. Not a big deal where we were going, Commons tend to sleep in a bit and should be flying well into the noon hour. They differ a little from Barrows in the Sound in the fact that the Barrows are pretty consistent the whole season. The Commons come a little later in the year and sort of trickle into the salt. Then, in what seems all at once, they are thicker than thieves and gang up in big rafts before they disperse into the fresh water lakes and sloughs most folks find them.

In Eastern Washington the big flocks arrive even later in the year, around early January, and follow the river systems to the lakes. I have seen some mighty congregations east of the mountains, easily twice as many as we get. The trade off though is they rarely if ever see many Barrows. I know my friend Brad Forgey, who is as ardent a Goldeneye hunter as you will ever meet, harvests about one Barrows for every nine to ten Commons a year near the Spokane area.

We arrived by boat to our spot with about a half hour before shooting. I was still carrying that confidence I knew something great was going to happen. Jason had suggested that Drewry joining us with Spence may just be that good karma we were waiting for and I couldn't argue that. That did make the day but there was a little voice telling me there was more. I just didn't want to say anything out loud to jinx the morning. What little I know about karma is that bragging about it can't be good.

Everything was going smooth. We set the lines from the shore and put out about fifty decoys. I walked down to the left side of the spread to check out Jason's new decoys. They were unbelievable, floating perfectly as designed. I really love his decoys and feel very fortunate to gun over such fine craftsmanship.

First light came and went with a few hen Mallards and a pair of hen Goldeneyes paying us a visit. The sun was trying to work itself out of what little clouds were in the sky. It was cold but dry with a slight breeze out of the south.

"You know Jay, that hen Common deke would be one fine Christmas present." Every year there are a couple things I can count on and getting a decoy from Jason is one I hope never goes away. "Those two hens sure like her. They think she is one of the gals."

"Just be patient there John, you never know what else may already be wrapped up."

A couple of minutes later I thought I heard the distant calling of Canada Geese. It wasn't uncommon for us to shoot a couple every year at this particular beach. The best part about the Canada's that fly by is that a good portion of them are the sub species Vancouver from the large-bodied group. Most Vancouver's winter north in Canada on Vancouver Island except a small population that migrates to Port Susan in Washington and another small location in Oregon. We were set up about a mile away from the protected reserve in Port Susan where they go to rest and get away from gunning pressure. Every now and then a few will leave the comforts of the reserve. The beach we were hunting on today is private giving us one of the only chances in the state to harvest this goose. We have been hit up by collectors for hunts here but the odds of actually getting a few to cooperate on command are slim to none.

"John, do you hear that?" He whispered over to me.

"Yeah, and they are getting closer, do you have your call?" The moment I said that Jason started a mad scramble. I looked up and finally saw the flock. They were coming right down the beach about twenty yards high and fast. The first group looked to be about fifteen birds strong with a pair trailing behind.

"Jay, no need for the call, here they are!"

We both stood up as they crossed over head. It was clear the first flock was normal Greaters and they had no idea we were there. I pulled up on the last bird on my side and dropped him right on the beach. As I followed it down I could see Jason had geese falling everywhere. I quickly looked for another shot and notice the two trailers trying to get out over the open water. It was clear they were Vancouver's; their dark bellies were giving them away. I drew a bead on the left bird and broke a wing. It wasn't hit very well so I used my last shell to clean it up off the water letting the other fly off to safety.

Jason started to dance around as he was picking up the last bird of his triple. "Yes! I got a band!"

"No way!" I yelled in disbelief. "Our first goose band!"

I ran over to meet him to inspect the jewelry. It looked a little worn but very readable. This was his second band this year and one of the rare times I have heard or seen of a Canada goose band harvested on the west side of the mountains. Now this was good karma.

"How'd you do? I was too busy chasing my birds down the beach to notice." The tone in his voice was still very shaky with excitement. I pointed at my Vancouver and we waded out together to retrieve it. Not quite a band but to me even better. As a taxidermist my one goal on every hunting trip is to get one good skin. I had better than that; I had a rare Vancouver specimen in excellent condition.

As we settled back into the blind I couldn't help but shake my head. Luck was on our side once again. No goose decoys, no calling, and they came over us at fifteen yards tops. I was just hoping we could extend this to include Dave who was still about a half hour out.

We didn't have much time to relax as the Goldneyes started to show up. The weather conditions were perfect to hear the whistling of the wings at full volume as they came screaming into the decoys. I picked up the first drake and Jason got the next two. My second bird came in from behind, a fully plumed bull Lesser Scaup that I was pleased to harvest over salt water. We were having a wonderful shoot when we saw Dave and Spence paddle around the corner.

"Good sign, I see plenty of birds moving. How you guys making out?" Before Dave finished this sentence I could see Spence had noticed the honks on the log and was staring wide eyed.

"Not too bad, a few whistlers, a bill, and oh yeah, a wad of honks and a little piece of jewelry!" Jason boasted. Dave hurriedly beached his Pod and the two Drewry boys rushed over to see our good fortune.

"Dad, I think Mom would be happy if we brought home a Christmas goose, can you shoot one for the family?" Spence asked in a way of total confidence in his Dad.

"We'll see Spence, you never know." He answered while giving us a snide look of doubt. "Maybe the Otto's will let us take one of theirs?"

Before I could answer affirmatively on that question Spence said rather seriously, "No Dad, we have to shoot our own. It's our job to bring home dinner." I love the mind of a six year old and he has always been a pretty serious kid with some rather strong convictions. And besides, he is right, men bring home the meat. It's our job.

Dave leaned over to me and whispered with a chuckle, "Well, let's test that little karma theory of yours, eh?"

The whistling of another drake coming near had us scatter back to the blind. Dave was ready to go and we wanted him to catch up on the ducks. It was a solo and totally committed. He waited for it to clear the last part of the long line holding a few corkers and sent him tumbling into the water. As he stood up to walk over for the retrieve a pair came from the opposite side a little higher than we normally see them decoy. He plucked the drake away from the hen and sent him splashing down.

One by one our birds piled up on the log until we all three shot our limit. Spence did most of the retrieving having no problem wading through the water and sloshing around on the beach. He was outfitted from head to toe with nothing but the best of gear. I didn't even know they made neoprene waders that small. Along with the Commons we managed two Barrows, a Gadwall, and a couple more Lesser Scaup. I picked up one of the Goldeneyes to inspect his plumage. All the birds were in prime shape, from their dark green iridescent head down to the jet black feathers of the tertials. I noticed one drake had a few black specs in his white circular cheek patch as did one of the crescent shaped Barrows. The others were stark white and clean. It was a good shoot.

There was still a little time left on all of our curfews but we decided to pack it in to make some points at home. We were all fully picked up with boats loaded and ready to head out when all three of us watched in silence as a lone goose dropped into a cove about five hundred yards down the bay.

"Spence, you want to try and give it a go? I think we may be able to paddle over there and give it a good stalk." Dave said as he pondered whether or not to dig back into the gear he had just organized.

"Dad, we have to try, we need that Christmas goose!"

So off they went paddling in the Pod along the shore. We watched as they got further and further out of view. Once they got near the cove I could see Dave pull the small boat on the beach up to the logs of high tide. Then the two of them started to low crawl in the sand before they disappeared.

"There is no way they are going to get that goose, what do you think?" I asked Jason while trying to find them in my binoculars.

"Oh, I know they will. Care to wager?" he replied. I took the bet. I felt like I was testing karma. I wanted to see how far we could push this.

The suspense was over quickly. We couldn't see them but could see the goose rise up as it was flushed. It started to crash down before we could hear the shot. A few moments later we could see the two cresting over the beach with the goose held high in hand. They got their Christmas goose and even though I lost the quick little bet our streak of success on this day forged on. To add to the good fortune it was another beauty of a Vancouver, most likely the pair bird from my earlier harvest.

While heading back to the rig I said a prayer under my breath like I always do after this hunt, a thank you for the many blessings in my life. The most important prayers are for my family and the people I most care about. And who was I kidding? I don't believe in karma. I believe you make your own luck. I know where my bread is buttered and I always give thanks to Him who makes it happen.

When I got home I was surprised to find the house empty. The family was off running errands, and I wasn't even missed. This was a lucky day. So lucky I got time to take a nap.

Chapter 18

Brant on Samish Bay

  Currently there are two counties in Washington State where it is legal to hunt Brant. Pacific County is found in the south west part of the state and home to Willapa Bay. Black Brant that migrate down the coast to southern California make a stop there, and for about five days a year they have an open season. I have only hunted Willapa once as a guest and found it to be quite hit and miss. We mostly took care of the "miss" portion on that particular trip. I don't know too many people that actually hunt there but I know the harvest is mostly around a couple of dozen birds a year, hardly of any significance. The majority of our season takes place in Skagit County, towards the end of each hunting year. This season, which has been only reopened for less than twenty years after a lengthy closure, is dependent on the wintering population of more than 6,000 birds. This may seem like quite a small number, but with limited access and quite frankly limited interest, the harvest on a good season may only hit 250 to 300 birds. In the five to seven days it can be open, one storm can reduce the harvest on any given day to zero. It seems about every three to four years the population requirement is not met for one reason or another and the season is canceled. This can break the heart of the Brant hunter; at least I know it does mine.

What is unique to Washington is the wintering population of the Melville Island Gray Belly. Although not yet classified as its own species, it is entirely a different bird with its own characteristics. The Gray Belly breeds, as you might have guessed, on Melville Island in northern Canada. It is some of the most remote and barren land that you can imagine. Some head to Iceland and even Ireland, while most migrate right to our back yard in Skagit County. They are easy to identify in hand compared to our Pacific Blacks, and mostly resemble the Atlantic Brant. When banded the biologists refer to our Gray Belly as a hybrid between the Pacific and the Atlantic. I prefer not to shoot the Gray's when hunting if given the choice. I spend most of my off season raising money and awareness of this special little sea goose while being a Director for the Washington Brant Foundation. Jason, Ben Welton, and Drewry are also Directors and share my same passion for the enrichment of life for this fragile sea bird. The President and founder of the Foundation is Maynard Axelson who is also an avid Brant hunter. He has gone to Melville Island and brought back pictures of the rugged life they live while breeding there. I am always amazed anything can live in such a desolate area let alone breed. Maynard's total dedication for Brant is truly an inspiration. I have never met an individual so tied to the life cycle of a species of waterfowl. This man knows and loves his Brant.

One way Jason and I try to steer clear of the Gray's is by hunting on Samish Bay. Samish is one of two bays in Skagit County that the Brant populate. Padilla would be the other, and by far the most popular. For some reason Samish holds a higher percentage of Pacific Blacks and we like it that way. That and we just prefer Samish over Padilla any day of the week for a variety of different reasons. The south portion of Padilla Bay has a reserve that is home to a large sand bar which is perfect for their grit needs. On the bay there are stakes that mark the reserve which extends to the open water. The normal routine for some of the gunners on Padilla is to line up their boats to cut off the Brant as they head into safety. You can predict this flight on the low tide, when the best grit is exposed. I have been on this firing line in the past and I simply don't like it. The Brant will come in low on the water and as they get close will ascend high to avoid the boats and rigs of decoys before dumping back down into the reserve. This can lead to some pretty reckless shooting to say the least, basically hunts I don't want to be part of or even witness. On any given Brant day there will be twenty to thirty parties on Padilla, maybe more, with most of them crowding into each other and competing for the same flocks on this line. They can have it. I don't want to give the impression though that there is anything wrong with this style of hunting, it just does not suit Jason and I. I won't however defend the legendary lengthy shots that are sometimes taken. It also must be said that not all partake in this manner and the quite experienced well thought of folks that do prefer to hunt this line can do quite well. It is my opinion though that the Waterfowlers that move with the birds on Padilla fare much better than those that use "the line".

Samish, on the other hand, has a third of the hunters with twice the area to gun when you take the firing line out of the equation, much more to our liking. One of the exceptions is the long time club that sits on the end of Samish Island where they actually hunt out of a blind on a long sandy spit. This is quite unique in the fact that there are not too many places in Washington where you can gun Brant from land. Their success is dependent on the birds that flow from Samish to Padilla and fly around the spit to get there. A biologist has recently told me their harvest has been down in the last couple of years, and he believes it is because of a large white shed they built to house all their decoys and supplies that is located close to where they hunt. He thinks this shed is making the adult birds a little wary. Not sure if there is any truth to that, but I do find it quite an amusing little story.

The other exception, or watch out if you will, is knowing where all the private land is located. Samish is full of old shellfish rights, some folks actually own the ground under the water making a portion of the bay private property. Most of Puget Sound is public property and this is a rare situation of old rights grandfathered in. If you find yourself anchoring your boat on private ground it won't take you very long to find out, especially during the Brant season. Someone will be there to greet you rather quickly and will for sure show you some nice Washington hospitality.

Having hunted Brant on both Coasts and even down in Mexico, I would rate Washington Brant hunting as actually quite poor. I hate to admit this, and I am sure some of the die hard Brant hunters would take a little exception to that statement, but it is simply true. Maybe a better description would be that Brant hunting in Washington is the most challenging of the areas that I have hunted. After witnessing waves after waves of Atlantic Brant on the East Coast, and decoying thousands upon thousands of birds in San Quintin Bay in the Baja Peninsula, I may be a bit jaded. San Quintin Bay, for example, holds up to 60,000 Black Brant at one time and they seem to occupy every nook and cranny. This bay is not much bigger than Samish, and considering that Samish and Padilla are lucky to get 8,500 in a bountiful year, you get the point. A great seasonal harvest in Washington is three to four birds, and I know some that will tell you if you get any at all you are lucky. My highest harvest in one particular season is a mere three birds. What you do get in Washington is something else, more of a sense of accomplishment. Each harvest feels just a bit more special than those other places. Maybe it's the short season, or the small population of birds, or even the special waters that are hunted. A Washington Brant is really a harvest only a relative small handful of people get to experience. To me, that is what stands out.

Every year Dave, Jason and I pick a day or two out of the small season to target the Brant. I have yet to hunt all the available days and most likely never will. This is not the norm for most Washington Brant gunners; most will take advantage of every opportunity. I was once told by one particular old timer, "anyone crazy enough to take the time to build a rig of decoys for a bird that may or may not be open from year to year, better dang use them every chance they get!" I have to agree with that, but I AM a little crazy. I have no problem spending time and money on a rig that may see the water only once a year.

Our rig is sort of a mix and match of years of collecting. My favorite decoy is a cedar preening bird that Drewry made, cedar taken directly off of his property. It was made to look like it was carved over a hundred years ago, evoking the histories and traditions that seem to follow Brant gunning. Jason and I also have a matching pair made from turn of the century cedar telegraph poles that had long been retired. These were used for years by a club on the East Coast and given to us by a friend and fellow Brant hunter from New Jersey named Dave "Woody" Woodland.

We had met Woody through our friend Tom Matus, who along with Jeff Hajjar of the Sure Cycle company joined us on a Sea Duck hunt a couple of years prior. They were a really nice "thank you" gift for hosting them. Joining the other random corkers are our pride and joy, our silly wet rig. Jason cut out and painted a set of silhouettes from his own pattern which number about two dozen. We deploy these on our Sitting Duck Y-boards, the same set up we use for our Scoters. These decoys stand out for well over a mile on a nice sunny day, crucial when hunting limited amounts of birds.

The Sitting Duck Company is owned by our good friends and fellow carvers Jason Barnett and Cory Herendeen, who we have been lucky enough to have both hosted and shared a blind with. When added to the others it really gives the rig a "full" look. We got the idea while hunting near the Padilla firing line years prior and noticed on a slow day the only boat attracting birds were fellows who were using the large silhouettes. We have been hooked ever since.

Rounding out the rig when Dave joins us are his foam Herters decoys he received from his Grandfather who spent his winters hunting Brant in La Grulla located in Baja Mexico back in the 50's and 60's. These fakers hold special memories to Dave, and you can see it in his eyes when he pulls them from his slotted bags. I really enjoy watching the way those decoys effect him. The total amount we end up running is about six dozen, which I would say is average for the hunters in our area. There are larger rigs and even smaller rigs for sure, but six dozen is more than adequate.

This year opening day was on a Thursday and unlike other years, we were going. Normally we skip the first day to avoid the crowds, but since it was in the middle of the week we figured most would wait for the next available day which was a Saturday. We guessed right, when we pulled into the launch we were actually the first boat there. I was surprised by this but our solitude was somewhat short lived. Before we were moving to our spot there were four more trucks pulling up to launch. Even though our lease has a short list of members most are hardcore Brant gunners. On Saturday the number will easily double.

We were in Dave's boat which I always enjoy running on our side of the Sound. "Big Gray" seems a little out of place when she is not in her home waters of the Peninsula and we sure welcomed Dave handling the skipper duties. Bay dog also joined us, nothing like having a hardy Chesapeake retriever crashing the waves of the Samish.

They were calling for winds of 10 to 20 knots out of the east so we set up in a little protected area north of the launch protected by the foothills that ended at the shore. On the way we passed the old stilt blinds in the middle of Samish. I have been told they have stood there for over a hundred years. On a clear day you can see them from shore and they have become local landmarks. One of my favorite paintings on my wall is titled "Brant on Padilla Bay" by Cynthie Fisher which actually features these blinds. Too bad she painted them on the wrong bay! Our lease agreement allows us to use those but we never have. I would like to, someday, but for now we give way to the old timers that hold those in high tradition. They look a little worn and rickety, even a little dangerous. It would be worth it, though, just to partake in the history of those blinds. I can only imagine the hunts that have taken place there, the old bromide "if they could only talk" fits here quite nicely.

We set all the long lines and anchored the boat about fifteen yards off of the nearest decoy. Feeding and loafing Brant sort of take on the shape of a long windy road with the birds all clumped together. We emulated that and tried to position the boat to cut off any bird following newly paved water "road". Knowing the birds wouldn't really be moving until the low tide that was taking place about noon, we settled in for a long day. The chop was about a half a foot and we could see the rougher water to the west. First light was simply outstanding. The clouds in the skies were filled with a burning orange color that seemed never ending. A few Mallards buzzed by, then a few Widgeon, all a bit out of range and scattered. Our first locked and loaded customer was a nice drake White Wing Scoter that Dave promptly dropped right in the middle of the rig. Bay hit the water and just like that we had blood on the bow.

Out in the middle I could see some small flocks of Brant trading north and south. A few would leak out and run the tip of Samish Island on their way to Padilla, or the waiting guns of the club. On a flat calm day you can hear the distant shots from the public puddle duck grounds of the Welts unit in the upper Padilla Bay marsh. Not today, the only shots that we could hear were from the boats sharing Samish with us. I would guess there were about ten total on the water, really small for opening day. In the distance you can see the oil refineries that are on the west side of Padilla. The old timers use the smoke stacks to gauge the wind out over the bay. When I was growing up my Dad used the same trick with the stacks at the old Warehouser Mill in Everett near Possession Bay when he wanted to go Salmon fishing.

The whistle in the wings of a drake Surf Scoter winging by the decoys brought me out of my day dreaming. Jason pulled up and sent him crashing into the water. Following him was another trio of Surfs that Drewry was all over. He picked up two drakes himself on a nice double, and once again Bay was sent to work. The reports of the guns sent a small flock of Brant that had slid in behind us about five hundred yards scurrying for safer waters. They were close enough to hear the "glick . . . glick . . ." sounds of their calls. This perked me up and reminded me why we were here.

After a couple of hours of watching mostly Scoters and Buffleheads descend on the dekes we started to notice the tide was beginning to drop. You can always tell by the way the mother lines will drift because of the extra line due to the dropping water. I had picked up a couple of Surfs myself and a really nice Oldsquaw that dared to venture too close and was already quite satisfied. I was at the point that if we did get a shot at a Brant, it was now a bonus. You sort of have to treat Brant days in Washington like this at times. If not, you could really be setting yourself up for disappointment. The dropping tide meant the Brant were more apt to move, if we were going to be successful it would be in the next hour or so.

To the north, Jason pointed out a flock. We had seen a few movements from this area, but none of them had given us a second thought. This flock was acting different. Watching a flock of Brant is almost like watching a butterfly. They move in erratic groups, fluttering this way and that way in unison, almost on a whim. I didn't start getting excited until they were about two hundred yards out and now appeared to be heading straight for us.

"Glick . . . . glick . . . . glick . . ." Dave started to mouth call. That is something I haven't quite yet felt comfortable doing so I let him have all the fun. They started calling back and I knew then we were in business.

When they hit about fifty yards, the ten bird flock split with both heading towards the opposite ends of our rig. Not the way we had planned, but does it ever? I was sitting on the right side of the boat and concentrated on the four birds that were now right out in front. The first shot came from Jason who was sitting in the middle and I could see one of my four crumple into the water. I picked the lead bird, bore down, and smacked him. In that split second I realized I had a bird down I switched to the bird behind him and pulled the trigger. Two birds down! The last bird flew off untouched.

I quickly looked over to the other side of the rig to see two birds belly up. Jason had switched to the other flock after downing the first bird and had dispatched another bird on the other side. Talk about a tough double! Dave also had a bird down but couldn't take his second shot because the remaining birds had grouped too tight on their way out. Just like that Jason and I were limited and Dave only needed one more. Bay so excitedly jumped in the water from all the commotion she totally submerged herself on impact. She made quick work of the retrieves and we were left to admire our harvest.

All five birds were Pacific Blacks. Remarkably, only one was a juvenile and the other four were very nice mature adults. I had the biggest one of the group, an obvious bull male. Still shaking from the excitement I laid down my two birds and preened all the water off for a nice picture. The Blacks have the largest white ring of all the Brant and their dark bellies really leave no doubt of what you have in hand. Dave immediately started talking about the feast that we were planning if we were to be successful on the water. Brant are among the finest of table fare of all the waterfowl and rank right up there as our favorites with Canvasback and Teal. I just couldn't wait to mount the big bull I shot and I already had the pose in my mind.

It was almost close to noon and we made the decision to stick it out and try to get Dave his last bird. About an hour later a pair of Pacific's completely locked into the decoys and Dave made a solid shot to finish his limit. Still not wanting to leave, we stayed another couple of hours and ended up filling our Scoter limits. Much to Dave's delight Lady Luck shined on him once again and his last bird was a Black Scoter, a very rare bird for the area. This gave him the coveted "Scoter Slam". Normally this event would take center stage but not today. This day belonged to the Brant and we couldn't have been more elated.

After the long day on the water we decided to drive over to the launch to check on the Padilla hunters. It was getting late but there were a few still out there and a couple just coming in and were milling around. Per usual the results were mixed, some had great success, others had to be content with a fine day on the salts. We learned there were about fifteen boats total for the opener, one of the smallest crowds that I could remember.

That first flock summed up hunting Brant in Washington to a tee; you may only get one flock so you better make it count. I had to laugh as I remember looking out over the decoys and seeing all that fine craftsmanship. They represented a lot of time, money, and effort, all work that could be theoretically put into something else. Was it really worth all that for the hopes of getting one flock to cooperate? Is it worth it to plan on spending an entire day on the water knowing that most of it will be spent idle? Sometimes braving stout winds and heavy seas, most often than not coming up empty? Heck, are we even going to have a season? To any true Brant hunter those questions are about as stupid as it gets.

Chapter 19

Oldsquaws in the Layout

"Two birds, on your right. I think they are Surf's can't tell for sure."

I slowly turned my head and there they were. With my left hand I squeezed the two-way radio.

"Jay, it's a pair of White-Wings," I whispered, "here they come."

The two birds skirted the outside edge of the long line and headed to open water.

"John, there is a trailer!"

"I see him!"

I sat up from the layout boat to see a locked and loaded drake Surf Scoter about three feet above the water maneuvering for a place to land. He was maybe ten yards away. I drew a bead with my Benelli and pulled the trigger.

"Nice shot!" was heard over the radio.

In the distance I could hear the hum of the outboard as Jason came in with the tender. I had drawn first shooter this morning and we were hunting out of a Mighty Layout Boy's Classic style layout boat. Still sitting up I could barely turn enough to see him motor up from behind me. When he got close to the rig I could hear him send Ruddy and the following splash as she swam to get my dead drake Surf.

"That bird would have landed on me if I hadn't shot it!" I yelled over to him as he got the bird and Ruddy into the boat. I was still pretty excited.

"Just let me know when you are ready to switch out," Jason replied. "I would be more than happy to take over your tough job!"

"Not yet, not yet . . ."

I lay back down and tried to get comfortable. I am not a tall guy or even a wide guy but these boats are made to get you as low to the water as possible. To do this all fringe space is eliminated. On the sides I barely have enough room to move my arms and when I stretch my neck to look down I can just make out my two feet that are turned sideways to fit into the front. When I look to my left and right all I can see is water, and it is right there, I am only inches above it. The perspective from this view is unbelievable and defies all other definitions until you experience it for yourself. The slight lapping of the waves on the sides will lull you into a sense you are not just in a boat, you are the boat. You feel every little bob in the water, every little breeze. To the birds you simply disappear into the sea of gray. This creates some of the most up close and personal gunning imaginable.

Off in the distance I could hear the calls of the Oldsquaws as they began to assemble, which is a common practice when in their country. I was set up in a channel of water about eighty feet deep. The Squaws will play and frolic out in the open waters, before they group up into parties of ten or so and work their way in to feed. Even the channel I was sitting in is about five hundred yards offshore. Being that far from land in such a small boat isn't for everybody and can be a bit unnerving, but I sure love it.

A trio of birds was coming directly in so I slowly moved my left hand to the forearm of my gun which was lying across my chest down to my waist. I could tell it was Squaws, two drakes and a hen. My lips were dry from all the salt water spray but I managed to give them the best mouth call I could muster.

"Oww . . . oww . . . lee! Oww . . . oww . . . lee!"

The three birds gave me a call back and landed just outside the rig. Behind them was a lone single. He over shot the swimmers and locked on the spread. As I pulled up I saw him throw his head backwards almost level with his tertials and give out the loudest call he could scream. He was coming in and he meant business. My first shot folded him cleanly about fifteen yards from the boat. The shot sent the trio in a confused flight, right to my left at only twenty yards away. I quickly turned and fired at the middle drake dropping them both. The unscathed hen did a loop and flew right back into the decoys and landed. The back drake was crippled and dove immediately while the other was lying on his back feet up. I had tripled on Longtails but I wasn't happy yet. A crippled Squaw is the hardest bird to clean up and their skill of diving and snorkeling out of sight on even the slightest of ripple in the water is matched by none.

"John, on my way! Any crips?"

"Yeah, I got two dead and one diver, he hasn't come up for a while, you need to hurry!" I answered. I knew the longer it would take for him to get there the more my odds will go down of getting that bird. Loosing an occasional cripple while sea duck hunting is a fact of life, it is going to happen, but it doesn't mean you have to accept it or not give every effort possible. Being in a layout boat renders you helpless, you need a good tender just for these occasions.

While waiting for the bird to surface I noticed out of the corner of my eye the hen pick up and take off. Jason was coming and he ripped past me out into the open water. I didn't know if he had seen the crip but he looked like he was on a mission. About a hundred yards out I saw him put the boat in neutral. He slowly stood up and took a shot. I saw the spray of the water lift high into the air well before I heard any of the noise. It became quickly obvious he got the bird as I watched him reorganize the boat before he threw it back in gear. Seeing him swoop down and pick something out of the water gave me a great sense of relief and I could now enjoy my triple. The current had swept the other two drakes out of the decoys and about forty yards behind me, it had quite a rip.

"Nice birds, you got some sweet tails. I think the one I cleaned up has to be at least ten inches long," he said as he pulled up near the layout to show me the birds.

"Oh man, I am still shaking. That was exciting. Thanks for the back up, it was sort of a scotch doubled triple, but I will take it! Ready to trade out?"

"Not yet," he replied, "get one more bird first. You haven't been in there but twenty minutes. I'm having fun watching the action."

I wasn't going to argue.

The next bird to come in was a hen Surf who danced around the lines and landed. While being totally oblivious to me she began to swim right up to the boat. I felt like I could reach out and grab her. Before I knew it three more Surfs ripped right over my head and joined her. They flew so close I swear I got brushed by a wing tip. I let them play and frolic right in front of me for quite some time, nothing like live decoys.

A SEASON OF WING-SHOOTING

From far out I could see something coming that at first looked like another Squaw. As it got closer I could tell it was a prime drake Bufflehead. He came in low and fast, right above the decoys so close I couldn't shoot without putting pellets into cork. I passed. He then doubled back and circled in behind me. As much fun as a layout boat is to hunt from it is unforgiving for anything behind you unless you have the talents of a gymnast. Finally, he presented himself right out in front while flying out. It was a tough shot but I sent him into a tailspin down to the water. This once again prompted Jason and the boat and I knew he had seen enough.

"I thought you would never get a shot at him. You ready to stretch out?" Jason said as he pulled up the boat along side of me.

"I think that little Butterball wanted to make a pretzel out of me!"

I handed him the belt PFD and in he jumped. It did feel good to stretch out the feet and arms but I could have stayed in there for hours. I ran the boat down to the buoy he had set up and started watching the show. Seeing the layout from my new view puts a whole different perspective on the hunt. Jason seemed so tiny in such large water. Watching birds decoy now looks like they are pulled in by some magnetic force.

"Holy cow, did you see that hen? She almost took my head off!"

I answered Jason back on the two-way, "Welcome to the layout!"

I finally got to inspect my birds for the day. The Squaws were in perfect plumage. The black lines of the breast feathers were crisp and the grays of the flanks and tertials were lined with silver tips. Two of the three had about eight inch tails which is about normal. The one did have about ten inches and it was just flowing in the wind as it pointed upward. The largest tail I have ever seen or shot measured at eleven inches. I would be hard pressed to believe there are thirteen or fourteen inchers out there as some people claim, but it is like anything else. I have seen a lot of thirty pound salmon go eighteen if you know what I mean. The Buff was a beauty; it had a really nice set of head feathers full of iridescence. The black of the Surf gave my little row of birds some nice contrast and it was a good looking brace.

Three shots quickly came from Jason. I looked up to see a lone White-Wing Scoter flying out of the rig and headed towards safety.

"What happened Jay? How did you miss?" I inquired over the radio.

"Miss? Get over here and pick up my bird! I dropped the drake and let the hen go."

I totally missed that. I threw the buoy and started the outboard. Another shot ripped and this one I caught, Jason had another bird down. When I got there I saw he had shot his first Squaw belly down. It was a huge bull and I could tell we had another ten incher.

"Sweet! I saw that one fall. Looked like a close shot!"

151

"Oh man, it was. It was a little to my left, I had to put the butt of the gun on my bicep, and let me tell you, that hurt."

We both had a good chuckle about that. Such is the way of the layout shooter. At times you just have to improvise and take the best shot the best way that you can. It is all part of the challenge. Believe it or not, it is much harder to hit a bird at ten yards than at twenty. The closer you take your shot, the tighter your spread.

Layout hunting did not develop to make hunting easy. It was mostly evolved from the Waterfowlers of yesteryear while trying to get away from everyone else that lined the beaches. It is an effective and successful way to get to the open water for species that may shy away from the larger boat blinds. Getting birds in your face is nothing more than a fun, challenging byproduct.

We had the pleasure of hosting Mark Rongers, the founder of the Mighty Layout Boy's company, on a hunt and he was astonished at the lack of layout hunters in the Pacific Northwest. He made an observation and what I think is a valid point, the more pressure our area receives as they choke down our public lands, the more folks will be forced to find new ways to get away from the crowds.

Open water hunting and layout hunting will gain in popularity out of sheer necessity. Basically the Midwest and the East coast layout style of hunting is part of their past and present while in the Northwest and West coast it will be part of our future. A future that very few of us are lucky enough to be enjoying right now.

The rest of the day was spent trading in and out of the layout until we both got our birds. I picked up my fourth Longtail shortly after Jason got all four of his. Our season is starting to wind down and it felt good to get in a quality layout shoot. Thinking back on a drake Oldsquaw with his head thrown back screaming his way into the decoys will give me chills that will last throughout the off-season.

Chapter 20

Beach Hunting Bills

Tomorrow is the last day of the season, and I am exhausted. So was Jason. This day will be our ninth day in a row of hard core hunting, spanning four counties, three different bays, a river, two lakes, and a frozen field. This is nothing new for us, every year we average about 60 days on the water or in some old forgotten marsh chasing waterfowl. Considering Washington has a 107 day season, we often joke we barely hunt half as much as we should be out there! But nine days in a row take its toll and I feel like I am on auto pilot. Driving home after a successful Canvasback hunt we started to ponder our options of how to finish out the year.

"There were still lots of Can's in the area, want to do that again?" I threw out to Jason. It was a little bit of a selfish request and he knew it. Cans mean we could sleep in a bit and heck, the truck and rig was already loaded allowing time to crash when I got home.

"John, I need you to man-up. Hear me out. I want, no, I need to finish out on Bills. We haven't shot a single Scaup this whole week and it is killing me. What do you say?"

How could I say no to that? The guy had a point, and as much as I knew it was going to cost me, Scaup hunting is what I wanted to do as well. I was fully aware this meant switching out our entire gear, going from the Pods to our boat. It also would prevent me from any type of sleeping in, the spot I knew he would want to go to was at least an hour away on the bay. One more day I thought, and I knew I would be really pleased once that rig was out and I was staring down the barrel at a big pig of a Greater Scaup dive bombing the spread.

"You got it, and I suppose you want to go to "Driftwood Blind Beach", right?"

He laughed and just sneered a nod in my direction. I have to hand it to my brother; whenever something calls for a little extra work or drive he is always there to provide the charge. Nine days in a row, boy was I tired.

I got home and started to put away my Canvasback decoys. It hit me as I was wiping them down and putting them on the bench for their annual paint touch up that I was preparing for in the off-season. These decoys won't be used until next year. I felt destroyed, but a part of me felt a little relieved. Next Saturday I could sleep in, I could actually see sunlight when I woke up. That feeling of morning freedom would be fleeting, by the next Saturday I will have sunk into a deep depression. After all, the next couple of weekends would mark the longest part of the year until the season re-opens. I looked over at my bags of puddle duck decoys which were in use about three days earlier sitting in the corner of the garage. Little did I think they were done when I came home that day. Put away for the last time. I grabbed my Scaup slotted bags and got a little encouraged. The season wasn't dead yet and these boys still had one more day. I picked up a cedar Greater Scaup that Tom Matus had carved for me a few years earlier. His decoys always have so much expression and detail. I swear I could hear it talking to me, telling me "let's go get 'em . . ." I was feeling much better.

I didn't even hear the alarm go off. Toni leaned over and started to shake me.

"John, you better get up, you are going to be late."

"Oh man, I'm up, thanks." I staggered to the edge of the bed and just sat there in a daze. I remember the first get up in September going for grouse. I recall thinking that was the beginning to a long season of seeing 3:30 in the morning. I sure popped up fast that day and I am positive come next September I will forget all about this moment, I always do. This is nothing a couple of Red Bulls can't fix, I thought.

An hour later and we were on our way to the launch. I was now full of energy and anxious to get on the water but the drive was almost bitter sweet. For four months I spend hours and hours with my brother and almost see him on a daily basis. Most people would get sick of seeing the same person so much but not me, not at all. There are times we can get a little lippy with each other or a little frustrated, but it never lasts more than a few moments and we quickly laugh it off.

We are two peas in a pod, two guys who were meant to be together. Part of my withdrawals in the off-season will be missing him. There will still be our February scouting trips, days spent in the garages carving and doing taxidermy throughout the summer, but nothing to the extent I get to see him now. He is the best friend and hunting partner a guy could ever ask for. He has been there for every up down in my life and solid as a rock. I lean on him more than he will ever know. I am going to miss these morning drives. I can take solace in the fact I know we will be doing this every season until the day they take both our drivers licenses away when we are old and gray. God willing I hope we turn into two old codgers that people will point at and poke fun of, hoping we don't have a heart attack in the blind.

At the launch I got out of the truck and was hit in the face with a cold brisk northern wind. Driftwood beach will be nice and protected from this but the trick will be getting there. I could hear the waves before we got to the water. The bay had one to two foot chop and I knew it was going to be a "fun" ride. I should have known the last day was going to be work.

When you are on the water at night with sloppy conditions the weather is always magnified. If there were daylight the waves we were fighting wouldn't seem like much and the spray wouldn't be as cold. With darkness all around it gives the impression you are headed into the unknown. A little white knuckled action always gets the adrenaline flowing but truth be told I would much rather have a nice calm ride. I know my backside appreciates it as well. Sitting in the front of the boat can be rather vivacious. I always warn folks who are new to hunting the big water that it takes experience and knowledge of the salts to know when to go out or when to go have an early breakfast. Error on the safe side and don't learn in the dark. We felt this morning was manageable and took our time cutting through the chop making sure we were hitting the waves straight on and staying equal with the swells. After about two miles we reached the point and headed south west with the protection of the land. The water seemed to immediately calm down and relieved to be through the rough patch we were now able to cruise at full throttle to our spot. There is a street lamp on top of the cliff near the beach that gives a lighted path on the water to guide us to the beach.

Jason dropped me off and took the boat to hide around a little corner in the cove. The wind was still running at a pretty good clip to the north even though it wasn't affecting the water. The beach was made up of little pebbles and crushed clam and mussel shells giving it an almost black color. At the high tide mark were mountains of driftwood where we would make our blind, and how this beach got its silly Otto Brothers name.

Behind that is about 500 yards of pickle grass marsh with random logs that were trapped on past extreme tides. Beyond the marsh is a salt water lagoon of trapped water about a quarter of a mile long and maybe two hundred yards deep. This would be ideal to hunt but there are a few houses tucked into the woods on the far side and we don't want to be any where near these folks. We have often talked about asking them for permission to access this spot through their property but we have never seen any lights on during the winter. I think they are summer homes. Either way, it would sort of feel like cheating if we could simply drive to this spot and hike a couple of hundred yards. I like the boat ride and we have been hunting here the same way for years.

The back lagoon has a muddy silt laden bottom that is full of the small fingernail size butter clams the Scaup devour on a daily basis. It also attracts plenty of puddle ducks, Buffleheads, both species of Goldeneye's, Common and Hooded Mergansers, and the occasional Harlequin. When the tide is at a mid point the lagoon is once again connected to the bay and can fill the marsh from the back out as the tide increases. This morning the tide was low and on the rise with a high tide of about 11 feet in the afternoon. When it gets that high our beach is reduced to a thin strip resembling a natural dike. Walking the pickle grass on a low tide can result in multiple flushes of Snipe and on slow gunning days we have been known to pick up a few for the skillet. Last year I mounted a Snipe I took from here and was surprised at how durable the skin turned out to be. I really enjoyed the process and the resulting mount for the wall.

With the decoys deployed and the blind up and ready, we decided to take a walk down the beach to kill the twenty minutes we had to wait for the day to start. We were both on "shell patrol" looking for any unusual shells or neatly colored rocks for our girls. Having five daughters between us we couldn't just find one or two, it takes a blind bag full to satisfy that crowd.

"Last morning Jay. Soak it in."

"I was thinking the same thing. Remember this moment. We are minutes before our last hunt of this year. I don't know about you but I will think back to this moment all summer thinking I will do anything to be back here, right now."

Jason just stared over the bay as he talked. I saw him close his eyes and feel the wind. I did the same.

"Let's make this a good one. It's been a great season and I want to go out with a smile."

The fluttering of puddle duck wings making their way to the back marsh made us hustle back to the blind. The sun was slowly starting to make a presence in the broken clouds that the wind was quickly pushing through. The only flaw of this place is setting up with the sun in our eyes. The clouds were very welcome.

The action started immediately. We let the first few flocks pass through the decoys. It was still a little dark and difficult to see the drakes. A few Mallards dropped in to check things out and were allowed to leave. Later in the morning they won't be so safe but we were on a Scaup hunt and it didn't seem right until we had a couple of Bills in the bag.

"There's a nice flock John, heading straight in. See 'em?"

"Yeah, the lead bird is a drake, a nice one!"

I sat up and put focus on the bird right up front. It was obvious the small group had no intentions of checking out the decoys and was only using them as a safe passage to get into the back lagoon. The Scaup were about fifteen yards off the water and moving at breakneck speed. I gave about a two canoe lead and pulled the trigger. Seeing that I folded him I quickly scanned the now fleeing flock. The momentum of the bird I had shot carried him over the beach into the blind nailing me on the thigh. This startled me to the point I couldn't get another shot off, and wow, did it hurt! I put the gun down and jumped out of the blind to walk it off. I would later see that I had a bruise the size of a soda can that lasted almost a month.

"Are you O.K.?" Jason said as he followed me out to the beach.

"Yeah, I am just glad that didn't hit me in the head! How come you didn't shoot?"

He paused for a moment while I danced around like a fool. "You know, I don't know. I guess I was just caught up in the moment."

I made my way back to the bird to see a prime drake Greater Scaup. I was astonished to see how little damage was done to the bird considering how hard he hit. He was feather perfect without a speck of blood. It looked like I had scared him to death. I picked him up and just focused on his magnificence. Greater's are such a heavy stout waterfowl and this one was a lumper. His belly was pure white up to the crisp black line of the chest. I moved his wing towards his back to see the side pockets. They were white as well, flowing into the gray checkered vermiculation of his back. I placed him on the log behind me to let him cool down in the still crisp morning air. We went back to watching the spread but I kept stealing little glances in between the action.

The next flock was a little more cooperative. They came in from the left and swung behind us and circled the lagoon before they locked onto the spread. We both turned around to face them as they tried to cup over the blind. I could see the black and white markings light up as they set in the sun with a cloudless back drop. The scene resembled a painting over real life as this surreal moment unfolded. Jason shot first sending his first bird of the day crashing down to the pebbles of the beach. I picked a nice drake on the edge and made an easy shot landing mine right near his. I saw another drake and shot a second time but missed. In their confusion half of the flock landed in the decoys. I twisted around to see another nice drake swimming nervously away from the spread. He lifted straight up at about thirty yards out and before I could shoot Jason let one fly and knocked him back down to the water.

"Yes! Nice shot Jay!"

"Thanks, that's makes it a triple! I couldn't tell if you knew he was there or not?"

Sure enough Jason had two in the water to go with the one I saw hit the beach. I waded out to get the bird on my side with my gun in hand. When I was up to my knees I saw out of the corner of my eye a lone bird flying low and coming straight at me. I froze in place so I wouldn't startle him. At twenty yards I pulled up and shot completely behind the bird. I swung to catch up and again pulled the trigger. Nothing. I forgot to reload and only had one shell left in the gun! I turned to Jason feeling like an idiot only to see him doubling over in laughter. I was glad to see him having such a good time.

Our log was starting to look impressive. There were five drakes and all in prime plumage, all Greaters. Scaup are the staple in the diver hunter world and can be shot throughout North America. Even though the populations have shown sharp and steady declines throughout the country our Pacific Flyway Greaters have been steadily increasing each year.

In the west side of our state, Padilla Bay may arguably be the most popular place to hunt Scaup. Waterfowlers who frequent this bay have been complaining in recent years that they notice a decline in the amount of birds that winter there. This may be true, or may not, I couldn't be sure as I don't spend a consistent amount of time on Padilla but I can say with a certainty that the waters surrounding the bay have increased dramatically. We see more Scaup in the little nooks and coves throughout the Sound where we had never seen them before. A simple theory would be that as diver hunting continues to become popular in Washington, with a majority of the folks gunning Padilla for Scaup, the pressure has plainly dispersed the birds. The amount of hunters chasing Bills there have easily quadrupled in the last ten years, maybe even more. What ever the reasons, Jason and I have had a windfall of spots over the last few years and finding more all the time.

"Here you go John, small flock to my right . . ."

I peered over his shoulder and watched as they came into range. Behind the first group of around ten birds was another small flock of five. Their wings were so low it seemed as if the wing tips were hitting the water. They skirted the outside of the rig and looped left coming right over my shoulder. I waited until their wings were locked and let a shot fly at a drake who was over top the others. I broke his wing and he soared down the beach. The rest of the flock shot straight up trying to escape. I picked a drake that was towards the bottom and stoned him into the rig. I then jumped out of the blind and ran to the edge of the water. I couldn't see the first bird I had dropped, he must have dove.

"See him John? Do I need to get the boat?" Jason yelled while running the other way. He too had a cripple down and I could see his swimming the opposite way.

"Take care of your bird," I shouted, "I will let you know!"

No sooner than I said that the bird popped up and was looking directly at me. At only ten yards away I backed up so I didn't shred the Scaup to pieces. Luckily he didn't dive again and I quickly dispatched the cripple. A moment later Jason shot and cleaned his up in the same manner. That little bout of chaos had my blood flowing. I retrieved my birds and headed back to the blind. My second Bill was a first year drake ruining our little streak of prime bulls for the log. It was a prize in his own right, still showing the green iridescence throughout his head flowing to the black of his chest. His belly was a bit brown with juvenile feathers and the side pockets were completely brownish gray.

Just like that we were limited out, we had four drake Greater Scaup apiece. Normally in this spot we would have had more Goldeneye's coming in but we had yet to decoy one drake. Also absent were the Buffleheads. The puddle ducks that were everywhere at first light had moved on to greener pastures as well.

"Well, what do we do now? We still have three birds left to shoot, should we move?" I asked. It was the last day and it was only 9 in the morning. It was way too early to call it a season.

"I say we smoke a cigar, enjoy these birds, and move out to the open water and see if we can finish out on Scoters. There is no sense staying here, and I don't want to end just yet," he answered as he sat back on the log.

I agreed. We sat and hung out for over an hour. It was good conversation. We talked about our plans for the upcoming summer, discussed trips for next year, decoys, and just about every thing else. It was then that I told him the big news I had found out only two days before.

"Jay, guess what. You might want to sit down."

"Hey, this sounds serious, is everything O.K.?"

"Toni and I found out what the baby is going to be. It's going to be a boy. I am going to name him Jackson Riley Otto. I am finally going to have my boy."

As I told him this a tear streamed down my cheek. I had been waiting for the best time to tell him and that moment there on the beach seemed as perfect as any. He grabbed me and gave me a big hug and then shook my hand.

"Pretty soon there will be another Otto boy joining us in the blind, I hope you don't mind," I choked out.

"John, I couldn't be happier. Congratulations. I didn't think you had it in you!"

With that we both laughed and smoked another cigar. I couldn't help but think of the year prior being on that very same beach while hosting Mark Rongers and the rest of the MLB crew. We had just had a wonderful hunt and all of us were limited and relaxing on the driftwood. Toni called me on my cell to let me know she had miscarried her pregnancy and needed me home immediately. Stunned, I turned to Mark and explained to him what had happened. With no hesitation he put his hands on my shoulders and prayed for me, right there on that beach. It turned out to be one of the worst days of my life mixed in with the kindness of new friends. Jason missed that day, and I have always thought that to be a blessing. Here it was, a year later, and I felt a rebirth. I mentioned to Jason it would have been nice to have the MLB guys with us today. He agreed, and I bet with the way the Scaup were flying, they would have had to agree as well.

The rest of the morning was spent in Penn Cove on the north side of the bay long lining for Scoters. The Surfs were flying well and we picked up our last bird just shy of noon. This was perfect for a year end celebration lunch at our favorite watering hole, Toby's. In a tradition that had started back when we were teenagers we each put a shell in our gun and aimed towards the sky.

"Jay, I want to thank you for a great season. It was full of memories and wonderful times. In no time we will be shooting grouse! Thanks for being my best friend."

"Right back at you John. May waterfowl forever be in our decoys!"

And with that we both shot into the air at the same time. The season was over.

"I have just one thing to add," Jay said as he placed his gun into his scabbard, "Let's make sure we set up for Surfs first thing on opening day next year!"

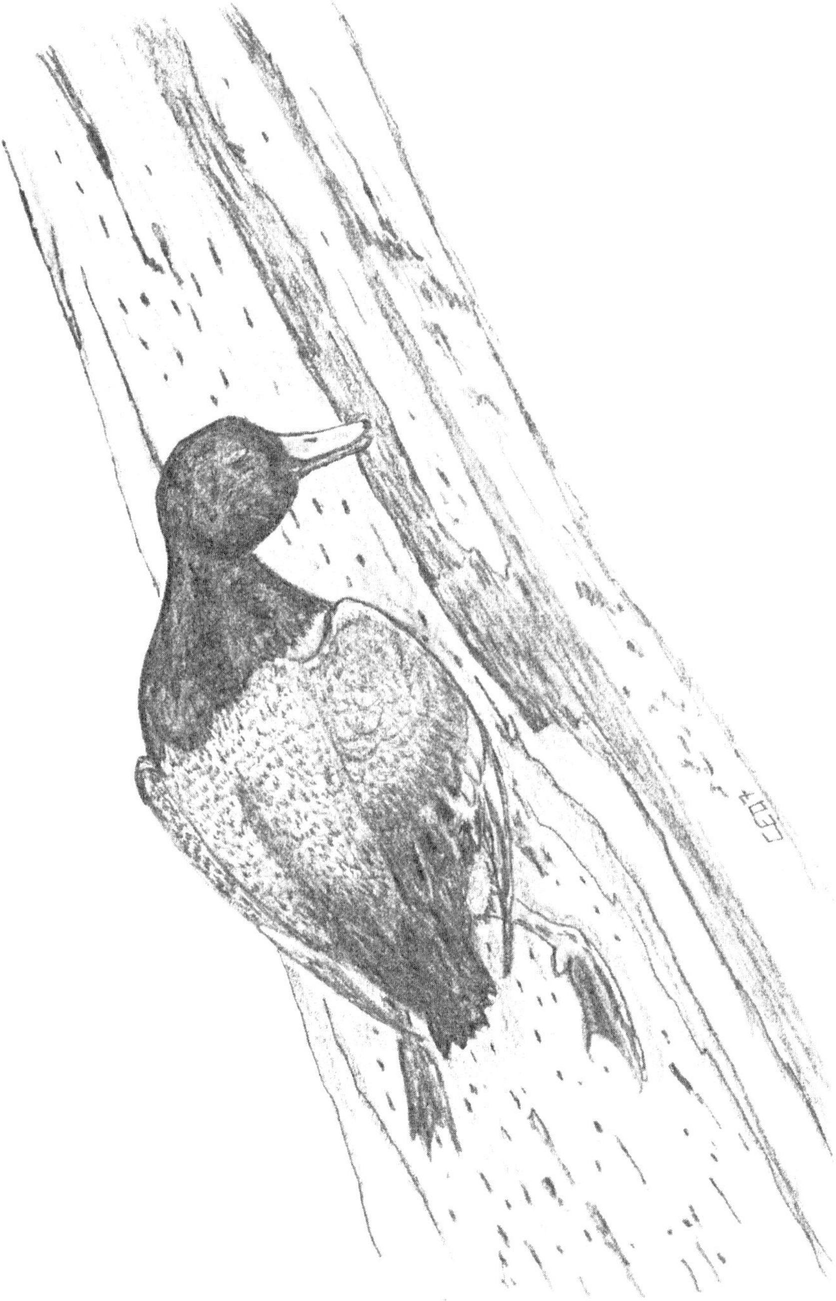

Epilogue

Jason Otto

When John took on the task of writing this book, he came to me and asked if I would do the honor of summarizing it, and write the epilogue. Bring it all to a nice little close. Maybe talk about a story or a situation that really captures what our partnership over the years has been all about. Being his brother, and also his best friend, it was quite a task. I battled in my head to find just the right words, the right mood to bring it all to an end.

I finally came to the realization that in order to have an end, you need a beginning. So what better story to tell than the first time we ever encountered a duck. The following is a story I will always cherish.

John and I are often asked how we got our start in hunting. Both of us will quickly agree that our Dad was the major influence and the sole reason for our passion for the sport. He was there from the beginning. I can not recall a time in my life where guns, dogs, or birds were not involved in some way. He started us early. I consider myself very lucky for having this upbringing, and am continuing our traditions with my own children, Chloe' and Natalie.

One story that John and I simply cannot agree on is the one of our first duck harvest. It was the fall of 1984 and we were pheasant hunting with our Dad in the Eastern Washington town of Royal City. John was fourteen at the time and already had a couple of years experience tagging along with Dad on these trips, with some limited success. I was only eleven and just starting to get my feet wet. It had been a long day of walking and there hadn't been many birds within shotgun range.

In fact, we hadn't fired a shot all day. We had just finished hunting yet another long draw. This one was thick with underbrush and native grasses, and after traveling its length, we had still not produced a pheasant. Looking back now I am sure Dad could see his two boys start to lose a little interest and we were getting tired from all the hiking.

"Hey, I know of a draw that leads down to an old swamp. It holds a lot of pheasants and from time to time has ducks on it," Dad said putting a little positive spin in his uplifted voice. I would later come to know this spot as the Fruit Stand, named by Dad and his long time friend and hunting partner Richard Green. "It will get us some birds, I promise!"

John and I were up for the adventure, but mostly because it meant we got to sit and rest awhile in the truck while he drove us there.

After a twenty minute drive that seemed like twenty seconds to me, we arrived at the famed Fruit Stand. John had been to this spot a few times before. For me, on the other hand, it was all new territory. I remember him telling me about it when he would come home from trips with Dad and Richard, the ones where I stayed home with Mom. For that whole twenty minute drive John was telling me how great this spot was and how he had bagged a pheasant there on a previous trip. His excitement had me sold, and I forgot how tired I was. Thinking back on that moment gives me a chuckle. John is famous for finding a positive in almost every situation; so much so that there are times I can't tell if even he believes it. I am sure this was one of those times, one of many to come.

We got out and loaded up the gear and got the guns. Dad went around to the back of the truck and got out his Labrador, Tar. If there were any birds to be found, Tar was the dog to find them. She jumped out and immediately started hunting. This got me really excited. I was hunting again and I loved it. Tar busted into the beginning of the draw and disappeared into the thickness of the cover. I could tell by the way the brush was thrashing that she was hot on scent. The adrenaline was now really kicking in, and I suddenly felt like I could hunt all day.

Dad and I were to the left of the draw. I could see just enough over the cover to spot John on the right. I remember looking up at Dad and seeing the concentration on his face. He saw me looking at him and flashed a big smile in my direction. That look said it all.

A SEASON OF WING-SHOOTING

"Get ready!" Dad barked out.

I looked down to see Tar only yards out in front. Before I could move, an explosion of color busted out of the cover heading right towards me and Dad. I froze.

"Take him! Take him!" Dad yelled, but I couldn't move. He realized I wasn't going to shoot so he pulled up and dropped him, stone dead. What I remember most was the excitement of all the commotion.

"Why didn't you shoot, Jay?" Dad asked with a big grin on his face.

"I don't know. I was just too excited!" As I told him this I was still trying to figure out all that just happened myself. At that point John had come over and put his arm around my shoulders.

"Welcome to pheasant hunting, Jason." Accompanying the hug was his typical big brother grin.

I remember Tar bringing back the pheasant to Dad. The sun was hitting the iridescence of the feathers just right. The colors were breathtaking. I was in awe. After a few minutes of sitting, admiring the bird and enjoying the moment, Dad gathered us up to show us the game plan on the upcoming swampy pond.

"Right beyond those cattails is the pond, "he said. He went on to explain to us (in his best hunting whisper) about how hunters jump shoot. He taught us how to walk along the cattails and cover, using it as camouflage, to make sure the ducks don't see us. I really enjoyed the strategy and the planning. It was one of those moments of learning that have lasted me a lifetime.

"I just know there is going to be ducks on there. Trust me guys."

Trust him we did. John and I headed towards the marsh beaming with excitement. The little huddle had us brimming with confidence and we knew something was going to happen. There just had to be a duck there.

John headed out first and I followed closely behind. He paused, slowly turned to me, and began to whisper. "Jay, let's start to crouch down here, sneak along this path by those cattails, and make sure you are being as quiet as you can." I nodded as I focused on big brother and his direction. I again have to chuckle as I remember this moment. It wouldn't take long before he started taking direction from me. Well, at least some times.

We sneaked together for a few hundred feet, all of which felt like miles, up to the ponds edge. Before we could even collect ourselves to make a plan a sweet little Green-Wing Teal erupted out of the cattails and into the sky.

From this moment on my memory is a little hazy. I remember pulling up and squeezing the trigger firing a shot. John did the same, simultaneously. The Teal was sent plummeting down to the water with as big a splash as the little bird could make. Dad immediately came up to the waters edge and sent Tar crashing into the water for the retrieve. I could see the "I am so proud" look in his eyes.

"Alright! Way to go!" He exclaimed as he put his arms around us. "Which one of you two got him?"

I looked at John and he looked at me. Both of us, without hesitation, said in unison, "I did!" Dad just smiled as he took the duck from Tar's mouth.

I can still remember the feeling of that afternoon. The excitement of the pheasant boiling out of the cover, Tar working the birds, and mostly the joy the three of us had hunting together. I didn't care who shot the Teal. It didn't matter to me or to John. We were both just happy to be out hunting with Dad and enjoying the great outdoors. We were hooked, and that is what it is all about.

To this day there are still some fun arguments over who shot that Teal. I don't think a hunting trip goes by where it doesn't come up. Dad always smiles and says he has no idea. But I know the truth. Not that it matters much, and in case you really want to know . . . it was me!

And I saw an angel standing in the sun; and he cried out with a loud voice, saying to all the birds which fly in midheaven, "Come, assemble for the great supper of God"

Revelations 19:17

Get Published, Inc!
Thorofare, NJ 08086
19 March, 2010
BA2010078